Junior NKIERE MAKOLONI

FIRST-YEAR COMPUTER COURSE SA

Junior NKIERE MAKOLONI

FIRST-YEAR COMPUTER COURSE SA

ScienciaScripts

Imprint

Cover image: www.ingimage.com

This book is a translation from the original published under ISBN 978-620-6-71276-3.

Publisher:
Sciencia Scripts
is a trademark of
Dodo Books Indian Ocean Ltd. and OmniScriptum S.R.L publishing group

120 High Road, East Finchley, London, N2 9ED, United Kingdom
Str. Armeneasca 28/1, office 1, Chisinau MD-2012, Republic of Moldova, Europe
Managing Directors: Ieva Konstantinova, Victoria Ursu
info@omniscriptum.com

Printed at: see last page
ISBN: 978-620-8-50934-7

Contents

PREFACE

Teaching a student who is starting his or her secondary education in Secretarial-Administrative studies the fundamental concepts of computing is one of the most important stages in his or her all-round education, with the aim of developing a spirit of initiative, creativity and responsibility and adapting to technical and technological developments, since secondary education is the link between basic education and practical life.

Its aim is to develop students' critical thinking, creativity and intellectual curiosity, and to prepare them for a trade or profession, or for higher education or university studies. One of the priorities for education, as decided by the Estates General on National Education, is to train children to acquire computer skills .[1]

Today's world is evolving at the pace of information technology and the Internet (information highways). All aspects of our society are governed by an organisation and administration based on information technology. Information technology, hitherto considered and used as a tool and support for certain subjects in national education systems, must become a real subject of study in its own right. And this teaching can only be done effectively on the basis of a well-written support by an IT specialist, while respecting the country's national curriculum.

The teaching of this course will lead students to adopt responsible behaviour and demonstrate practical life skills in relation to IT.

We would like to thank the Haut-Uélé Provincial Ministry of Education and the Haut-Uélé 2 Provincial Inspectorate for their involvement in the production of this book, which will be of use not only to Haut-Uélé Province but also to all the schools in our country that offer the secretarial-administrative option.

We recommend that schools fully appreciate the usefulness of IT tools and that they do more to unravel the mysteries of this new subject, which will turn Congolese children into responsible individuals who are useful to themselves and to society.

This book is not only useful for students, but also for teachers who want to learn computer science in the field of administration.

[1] **Constant N'DOM NDA OMBEL** ,*programme d'informatique de l'enseignement secondaire, 2007*,**p.2.**

SUMMARY

The IT sector attracts a large number of people who are looking for career guidance or retraining, because of the wealth and diversity of career opportunities it offers. The sector is constantly evolving, with plenty of scope for innovation and career opportunities. However, students need to be aware of the various disadvantages associated with this sector.

The aim of secondary education is to provide pupils with general and specific knowledge to enable them grasp elements of the national and international cultural heritage. It also aims to critical thinking, creativity and intellectual curiosity, and to prepare pupils for a trade or profession, or for higher education or university studies.

A student trained in secretarial administration is a professional capable of using IT tools to organise information, process texts using Microsoft Office programmes, print and use the Internet.

The writing of a book is a vital necessity in order to remedy the many problems and challenges, such as the lack of respect for the national curriculum of the computer science course for some, and the partial respect for this national curriculum for others, which proves a lack of professionalism in teaching, because the purpose of national education is the harmonious formation of the Congolese person, a responsible citizen, useful to himself and to society, capable of promoting the development of the country and national culture, responsible citizen, useful to himself and to society, capable of promoting the country's development and national culture (Loi-cadre n°86-005 du 22 /09/1986 de l'Enseignement National). The school must therefore train citizens who are productive, creative, cultured, conscientious, free and responsible, open to social, cultural, aesthetic, spiritual and republican values (Charte de l'Education, CNS, 1992).[2]

Students who have successfully completed computer training at secondary level will be able to handle the various operating system programmes (Windows) and Microsoft Word word processing applications.

[2] Designed and tested by **Junior NKIERE MAKOLONI**, Computer Engineer and Researcher, in compliance with the national curriculum of the Ministry of Primary, Secondary and Vocational Education of the Democratic Republic of Congo (DRC). Contact: +243 81087 0120, E-mail nkierejunior@gmail.com

OBJECTIVE

GENERAL OBJECTIVE

At the end of the first year of the Humanities secretarial administration, any student who follows this course assiduously will be able to type documents according to standards and use IT tools.

SPECIFIC OBJECTIVES

At the end of the first year of the humanities secretarial administration, the learner will be able to :

- organising information ;
- processing and entering data into the computer ;
- discover ms Word ;
- insert a WordArt ;
- present Excel ;
- print a document ;
- edit a Word document ;
- basic IT concepts ;
- know your computer ;
- use the internet.

CHAPTER I

INFORMATION ORGANISATION

I.1 FILES

I.1.1. DEFINITION

This is an organised collection of information, designated by a precise name, which the operating system of a computer manipulates as a single entity, in its memory or on a storage medium .[3]

I.1.2. FILE TYPE

In computing, in the world of Microsoft's MS/Dos and Windows computer operating , the type of file (its format) is given explicitly (in theory) by an extension to its filename, a suffix, commonly known as a "file extension".

OFFICE FILE

Here are the extensions for Office applications:

- **.doc**: version prior to Word 2007.
- **.docx**: Word 2007 and later.
- **.xls**: version prior to Excel 2007.
- **.xlsx**: Excel 2007 and later.
- **.ppt**: version prior to PowerPoint 2007.

1.1.3. FILE ORGANISATION

A file organisation is a way of arranging records in a file stored on disk. A file can be accessed and modified in different ways, and a file organisation can be good for one type of access and bad for another .[4]

1.1.3.1. PHYSICAL ORGANISATION OF FILES

Here we're taking a more macro perspective to understand how files are stored and organised physically on a storage medium.

1.1.3.2. FILE AND FOLDER TREE

On a workstation, you can find multiple **storage units**. Depending on the operating system, the way they are represented and named may vary, but the basic principles remain the same.

[3] https://www.futura-sciences.com, consulted on 20/09/2023 at 00:20'.
[4] https://www.labri.fr, consulted on 20/09/2023 at 00:24'.

Clicking on *Computer* will display the list of "visible" storage devices on the workstation. Under Windows, each is represented by a letter. At the very least, you will find the workstation's **hard disk** (here *C:*), which could be partitioned (i.e. split into several drives). You might also see **removable storage devices** such as a floppy drive or USB stick (here *D:*). Finally, there could be **network locations**, i.e. storage units accessible via a network (here *W:*, *X:*, *Y:*).

1.1.4. FILE MANAGEMENT

1.1.4.1. CREATING A FILE

Question: how do I create a folder within a folder? (You are going to create a folder with your first name in the ***My Documents*** folder**).**

1. Start **Windows Explorer**.
2. In the left-hand pane, select the **My Documents** folder with the following actions

2.1. in the left-hand pane, if necessary, display the folders contained in the **Libraries** folder (by clicking on the small triangle to the left of **Libraries**);

2.2. In the left-hand pane, if necessary, display the folders contained in the **Documents** folder (by clicking on the small triangle to the left of **Documents**); **2.3.** on **My Documents** to select this folder;

2.4. Note that selecting a folder in the left-hand pane has the following effects: (1) in the left-hand pane, the name of the folder is highlighted in blue and framed, and (2) in the right-hand pane, the names of the folders and files contained in that folder appear in alphabetical order;

2.5. Remember that when you select a folder in Windows, it tells Windows that the next actions will apply to this folder)

3. In the selected folder, create a folder bearing your first name using the following actions: **3.1.** On the command bar, click **New Folder** (the command bar is at the top of the screen and begins with the word **Organise**);

3.2. Note that **Windows Explorer** has created a folder called **New Folder** in the right-hand pane;

3.3. Also note that the words **New Folder** are selected; this indicates that, if you write words on the keyboard, these words will replace the words **New Folder**;

3.4. Write **your first name** (note that your first name automatically replaces the words **New folder**);

3.5. press **Enter**.

4. Close **Windows Explorer by** clicking on the small **X** at the top right of the window.

CHAPTER II

PROCESSING AND ENTERING DATA INTO THE COMPUTER

11.1. DATA COLLECTION DEFINITION

Data collection refers to the systematic approach gathering and measuring information from a variety of sources in order obtain a complete and accurate picture of an area of interest.[5]
Collecting data enables a person or company to answer relevant questions, evaluate results and better anticipate future probabilities and trends.

11.2. DATA COLLECTION METHODS

Surveys, interviews and interest are the main instruments used to gather information. Today, with the help web and analytics tools, companies can also collect data from mobile devices, website traffic, server activity and other relevant sources, according to the project.

11.3. TYPES OF DATA

Generally speaking, there are two types of data: quantitative and qualitative. Quantitative data is data presented in numerical form: statistics, percentages, etc. Qualitative data is descriptive data: colour, smell, appearance, quality, etc.

11.4. DATA ENTRY DEFINITION

Data entry involves collecting data and integrating all the information contained in a company document into an electronic device (laptop or desktop computer). The operation is carried out manually using a computer and certain software programmes. The data is stored in the computer's memory. However, for greater security, many companies are buying Cloud spaces in which they carry out their back-ups .[6]
Entering or **transcribing data** is a task that deserves serious consideration, as no errors or false information should be included in the database.

Types of data entry

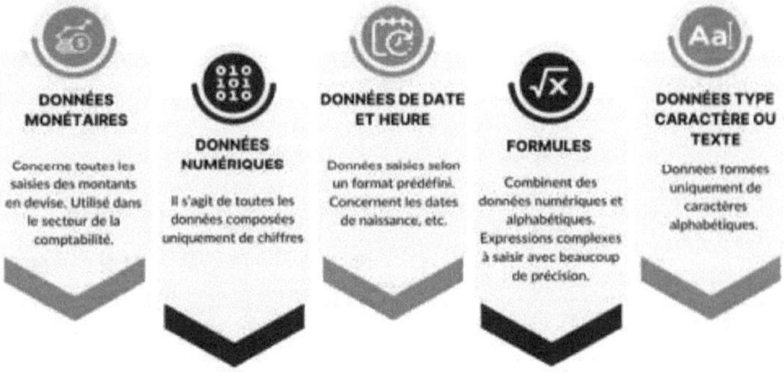

11.5. SOURCES OF COMPUTER INPUT DATA

Definition of data sources

A data source is the place where the data used comes from. A source of data can be the place where the data was created or the place where the physical information was digitised.

11.6. DATA ENTRY METHOD

Data capture is a process used to collect, record and organise information in a digital format. It is widely used in many fields, such as scientific research, market analysis, human resources

---

5 https://www.lemagit.fr, consulted on 20/09/2023 at 1h00'.
6 http://web.undp.org, consulted on 20/09/2023 at 1h20'.

management and many others. Data entry can be carried out manually or automatically using specialised software .[7]

11.6.1. THE DIFFERENT DATA ENTRY METHODS

There are several methods of entering data, each with its own advantages and disadvantages. Here are some of the most commonly used methods.

1. **Manual input**

Manual data entry is the process of entering data by hand, either on paper or on a computer. This method is often used when data is available in physical form, such as paper forms or questionnaires. Manual data entry can be tedious and prone to human error, but it offers significant flexibility and adaptability .[8]

2. **OCR input**

OCR (Optical Character Recognition) is a technology that converts physical documents into digital text. This method is often used to scan printed documents, such as invoices, receipts or contracts. OCR uses sophisticated algorithms to recognise printed characters and convert them into editable text .[9]

3. **Voice recognition input**

Speech recognition is a method of converting speech into text. It is often used to transcribe meetings, interviews or conferences. Speech recognition uses specialised software to analyse audio recordings and transform them into written text .[10]

4. **Automatic input**

Automatic data capture is a method that uses software to collect and store data from different sources, such as databases, websites or CSV files. This method is often used to collect data in real time, such as weather data or financial data .[11]

II.6.2. ADVANTAGES OF THE DATA CAPTURE METHOD

The data entry method has a number of advantages, including:

1. **Precision**

Data capture provides accurate and reliable information. By using specialised software, it is possible to minimise human error and ensure the consistency of the data collected.

2. **Time saving**

Automatic data capture enables large quantities of information to be collected and recorded quickly . This saves time and resources, eliminating the need for tedious manual data entry.

3. **Easy analysis**

Once the data has been entered, it is easier to analyse and interpret. Data capture software enables data to be efficiently sorted, filtered and visualised, making it easier to identify trends and patterns.

The challenges of the data capture method

Although the data entry method has many advantages, it is not without its challenges. Here are some of the challenges commonly encountered:

1. **Cost**

Setting up a data capture system can be costly, particularly if specialised software is required. In addition, training staff in the use of such software can also represent a significant investment.

---

[7] http://web.undp.org, consulted on 20/09/2023 at 1h29',
[8] https://www.yourtopia.fr, consulted on 20/09/2023 at 1h50'.
[9] Ditto
[10] Ditto
[11] Ditto

2. Data quality

The quality of the data entered can vary depending on the method used and the skills of the data entry personnel. It is important to implement quality control processes to ensure that the data collected is reliable and accurate.

3. Confidentiality and security

Data capture may involve the collection sensitive information, such as personal or financial data. It is essential that appropriate security measures are put in place to protect this information from unauthorised access or breaches of confidentiality.

Conclusion

The data capture method is an essential process for collecting, recording and organising information efficiently. It offers many advantages, such as accuracy, time savings and ease of analysis. However, it also presents challenges, such as cost and data quality. It is important to choose the data capture method best suited to your specific needs and to put in place quality control processes to guarantee the reliability of the data collected.

Questions and answers

Q : What is the best method for entering data?

A: *The best method of data capture depends on the specific needs of each project. Manual data capture may be more appropriate when data is available in physical form, while automatic data capture may be preferable for collecting data in real time. It is important to weigh up the advantages and disadvantages of each method before making a decision.*

Q : How can I guarantee the quality of the data I enter?

A: *To guarantee the quality of the data entered, it is essential to implement quality control processes. This may include the verification of data by several operators, the use of automatic validation software or the comparison of data with external sources. It is also important to train staff in data entry and provide them with clear guidelines on the quality standards to be met.*

Q : What are the advantages of automatic data entry?

A: *Automatic data capture offers a number of advantages, such as speed, accuracy and the ability to collect data in real time. It also saves time and resources by avoiding tedious manual data entry. However, it is important to choose reliable automatic data entry software and to put in place quality control processes to guarantee the reliability of the data collected.*

11.7. DETECT INPUT ERRORS

The input check is a very important stage any **data processing** operation. The contents of the files must be accurate, complete and error-free. Data entry checks are carried out in several stages, depending on the nature of the data to be entered and the type of error to be detected.

11.7.1. CHECKING THE VALIDITY OF ENTRIES

Input errors distort the result or render the calculation inconsistent or inoperative. Validity checks are used to avoid errors. This involves checking that the information entered does not contain any errors, such a non-existent order number or one that does not follow the logic. There are many software packages available today that allow users to check whether what they are typing is valid. Taking Excel as an example, the operator can, among other things, define a list of authorised values (whole numbers only, limit the length of text, set a minimum and maximum value to be entered, etc.). In this way, anything that does not respect the authorised values will be considered as an error.

11.7.2. DUPLICATE CHECK

Duplicate entries can be a source of error during data entry. So, before validating and saving the document, you need to detect any duplicate values. Excel allows you to perform this type of operation using conditional formatting and the duplicate search formula. Once the duplicates have been detected, you can delete them or correct them if they are the result of an error.

11.7.3. TEXT CONTENT CONTROL

Data entry also refers to purely textual content. For example, this might involve taking minutes at a meeting, writing a letter or transcribing audio or video. In these cases, spelling, syntax and grammar must be checked.

Text correction software should be used in this case. If this content is intended to be published on the website (product sheets, adverts, etc.), you need to check that it is not duplicate content. Google requires each piece of content to be original and relevant. That's why you need to use anti-plagiarism software.

11.8. STORAGE MEDIUM

I.PERIPHERALS

1. ***Input devices :***

They enable data to be entered and digitised (captured, recorded, scanned, etc.) so that it can be processed and/or stored on a computer.

Examples: Keyboard, mouse, scanner, microphone, webcam, joystick, barcode scanner, CD-ROM drive, DVD drive, optical pen, digital camera, ...

2. ***Output devices :***

They enable the output (display, projection, printing, audio, etc.) of information in a form that can be understood by the user.

Examples: Screen, printer, loudspeaker, video projector, plotter, etc.

3. ***Input/output devices :***

They enable information to be exchanged to and from a computer's central processing unit. *Examples:* modem, floppy drive, CD or DVD burner,

II. STORAGE MEDIA :

Storage media (mass memories or auxiliary memories) are physical media that enable data to be stored almost permanently. Some are housed in the enclosure's bays, while others can be hot-plugged or connected to an external drive (known as removable media).

1. ***Diskettes***

A floppy disk is a removable storage medium. It takes the form of a floppy disk on which data is written using a read/write head located on the floppy drive. There are several types of floppy disk, the main one being the 3" У2 floppy disk, which is 1.44 MB in size.

Production of the floppy disk has been discontinued since 2011.

2. ***The hard disk :***

A hard disk is a magnetic mass storage device used mainly in computers, but also in portable digital players, camcorders, home DVD players/recorders, video game consoles, etc.

The first hard disk was manufactured by IBM in the size of 5MO (1956) and today the size of a hard disk has reached 8TO (manufactured by Seagate in 2014). A hard disk is characterised by:

-1- Its storage capacity expressed in GB or TO

-2- Its density expressed in GB per tray

-3- Its rotation speed expressed in revolutions per minute

Its access time expressed in milliseconds
Its connection interface: IDE, SCSI or SATA
Its average transfer rate expressed in MB per second

Flash disk :

A USB flash memory drive is a small, removable storage device that connects to a computer's USB port. They come in different shapes and sizes.
This is the new generation of removable storage media, like an external hard drive.
It has the same characteristics as a hard disk.

The LASER disc (CD) :

This is an optical storage medium that comes in the form of : CD-ROM, CD-RW and CD-AUDIO... It has a capacity of around 700 MB (300,000 typed pages or 74 minutes of audio data).
It is characterised by its high data transfer time, low price and long life. It can be accessed using a CD/DVD drive or a CD/DVD burner.
^ *A DVD (digital versatile disc) has the same characteristics as a CD but is 4.7GB larger (1DVD ~7CD).*

The memory card :

The memory card is a non-volatile, rewritable semiconductor card. It is characterised by its durability, very small size and high speed. Memory cards are used in a wide range of applications (digital cameras, mobile phones, printers, laptops, MP3 players, etc.).

Magnetic tapes :

Magnetic tape (or magnetic ribbon) is a medium used for storing large quantities of information (archives) for a long time. From the 1950s onwards, tape formats became standard: a tape measured a maximum of 2400 feet long (732 metres) for У2 inch (127 mm) wide.

CHAPTER III

DISCOVERING WORD

111.1. LAUNCHING MS WORD

There are different ways of launching MS Word.

A. WITH THE START MENU

Note that the most conventional way of launching Word is to use the menu Start. Click succcssively on **Start> All programmes> Microsoft Office> Microsoft Word** (see figure below)

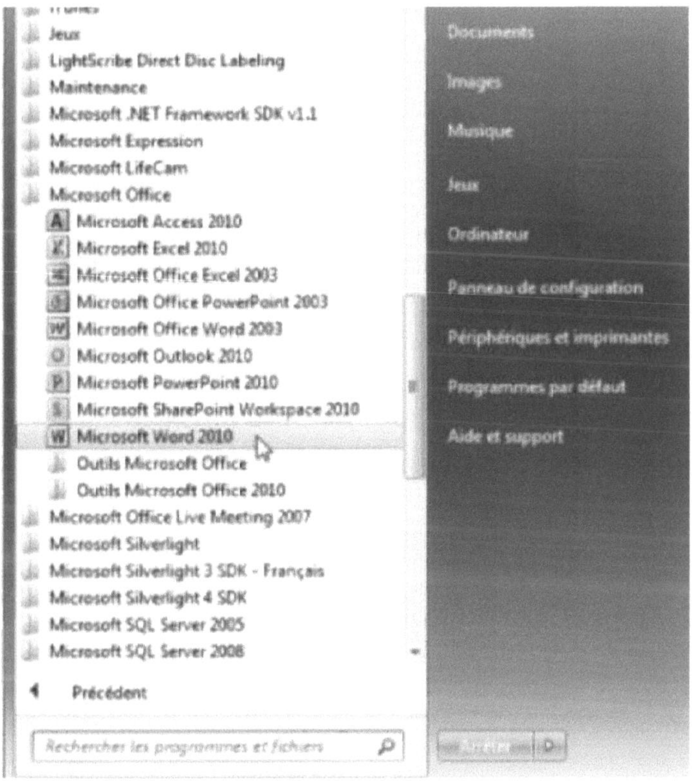

B. STARTING FROM THE DESKTOP

If there is a Word icon on the Windows desktop, you can double-click it to open the application (see figure below).

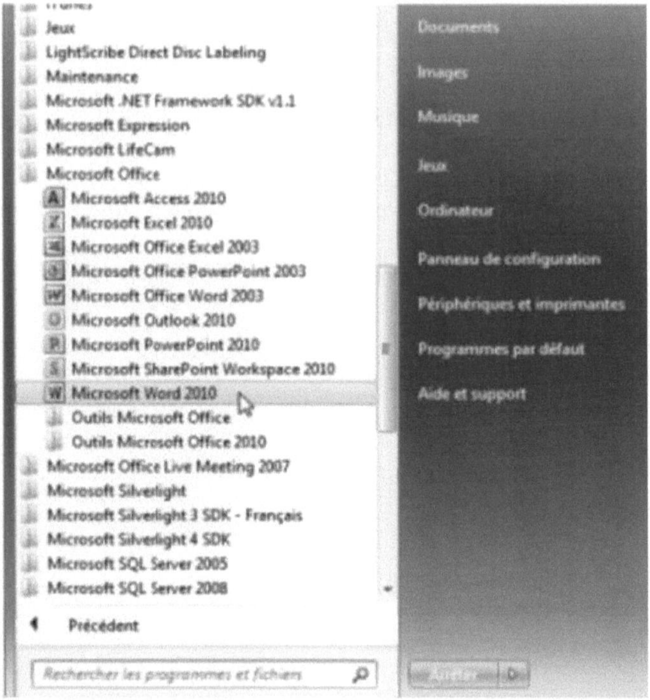

1.1.1. BRIEF DESCRIPTION OF THE RIBBON

To use Word properly, it is important to understand its interface, i.e. the various elements that make up the application window (see figure below).

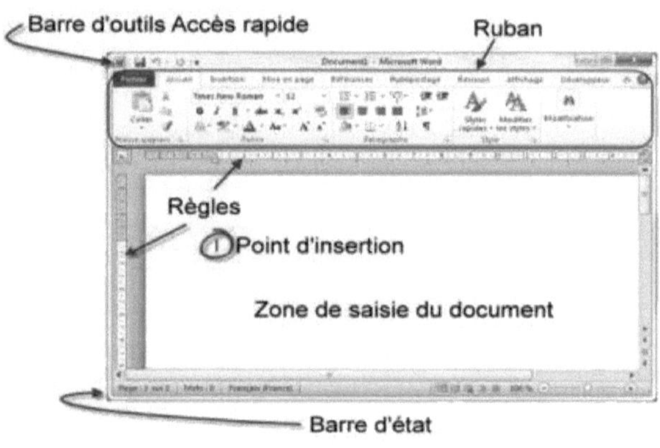

III.3. CREATING A NEW DOCUMENT

1.1.2. 1. NEW WORD DOCUMENT

The document entry area occupies the central part of the window. A flashing vertical bar, called the "insertion point", indicates where the next character typed on the keyboard will

appear. If the input area is not large enough to display the entire document, you can use the vertical and horizontal scrollbars to move around the document.
the document (see figure below).

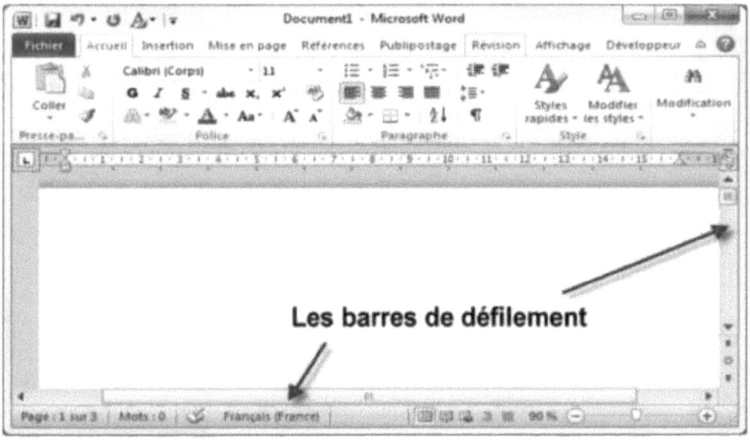

1.1.3. 2. DISPLAY OF THE RULE

You can easily display the ruler in Word and hide it. Microsoft Word provides you with a ruler that you can use to define tabs in a document.
To display or hide the ruler in Microsoft Word, first select the "**View**" tab in the Ribbon. Then check or uncheck the "**Ruler**" box in the "**Display**group to activate or deactivate the display of the ruler. Tick the box to display the ruler. Unchecking the box hides the ruler.

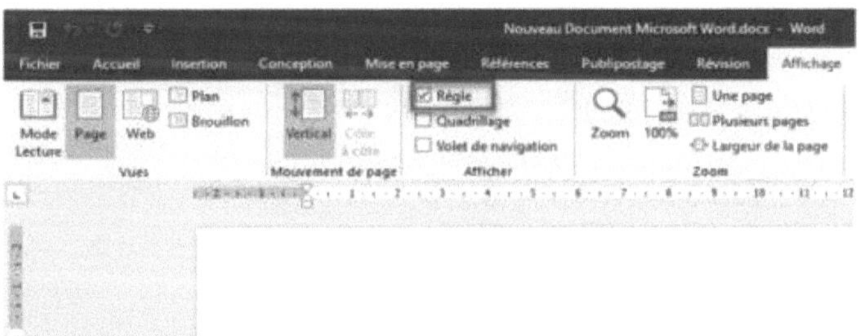

1.1.4. 3. TEXT INPUT

To enter text, simply type the required text into the appropriate part of the window. Unlike a typewriter, you don't need to validate at the end of the line, because the line break is automatic. Word takes care of this for you. This is known as "typing by the kilometre". You only validate when you want to create a new paragraph.
To create or change a paragraph, simply press the Enter key twice. The first time, you mark the end of the paragraph and the second time you leave a blank line between the two paragraphs. A paragraph can contain from zero to . ..many characters (a space counts as one character, the non-printable character representing it is a small dot.

111.4. OPEN, SAVE AND CLOSE A DOCUMENT

Allows you to access the software's general control and adjustment functions (saving a document, opening, printing, setting options, etc.). We use the office button for some offices and the File menu for others.

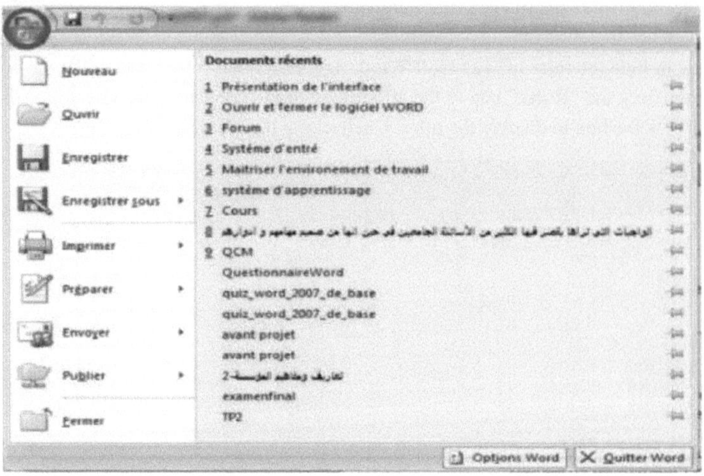

111.4.1. SAVING CHANGES TO A DOCUMENT

Once you have created a document, don't forget to save it, otherwise you risk losing all your work.

To do this, click on the **Office button** (or **File menu** for some offices) and then on the **Save As** button. You can then choose the save format:

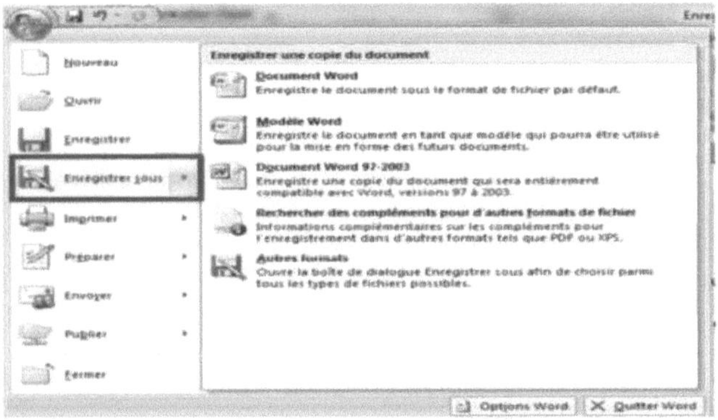

You now need to choose the location where you want to save your file, and specify the file name.

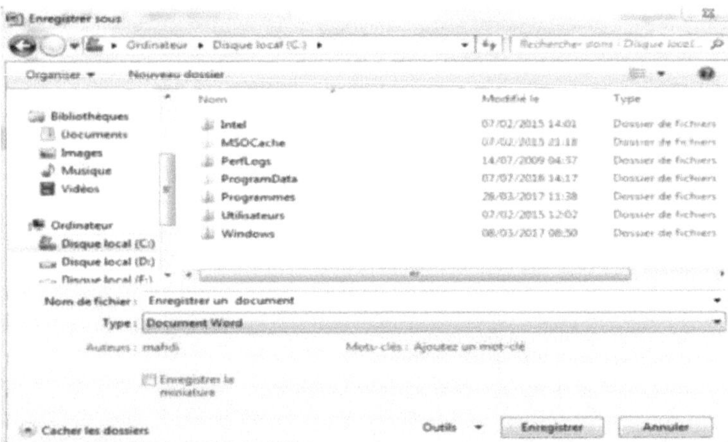

111.5. FORMATTING A WORD DOCUMENT

111.5.1. PARAGRAPH FORMATTING

As soon as you press the *Enter key* within a text, you create a new paragraph (empty, if it contains no characters).

There are as many paragraphs as ¶ characters (displayed when the "Display r" button is pressed).

all" icon is activated)

To change the *formatting of a single paragraph, simply place the cursor in that paragraph.*

If not, they need to be selected.

To format paragraphs, you can use :

- *The commands in the Paragraph group*, on the Home tab ;
- The *"Paragraph"* window that appears after activating the Paragraph group launcher ;
- *The mini formatting toolbar* ;
- *The horizontal ruler*. If it is not displayed: tick the "Ruler" box in the Show/Hide group on the View tab.

■ Or, more quickly: click on the tooltip button at the top of the the vertical scroll bar.

Withdrawals

There are 4 types of indentation, 3 on the left which correspond to the symbols: - on the ruler and one on the right :" .

a) Left indent (i.e. space left on the left, in addition to the margin)

There are three types of left-hand withdrawal:

- *Global indent* (for all lines): click and drag on the indent - on the ruler. The text is aligned with the dotted vertical line.
- *Indent only the 1st line of each paragraph*: click and drag the indentation on the ruler. This formatting is frequently used.
- *Indent all lines except the first line of each paragraph* (opposite to the previous case): click and drag on the "left indent" of the rule.

b) Right indent (i.e. space left on the right, in addition to the margin)

This time, use the right-hand indent ~ of the rule.

If you find that setting indentations with the ruler isn't precise enough, use the "Paragraph" window: right-click on the selected text > Paragraph > "Indent and space" tab.

Or, more quickly, *double-click on one of the 4 indentation symbols on the ruler*.

c) Decrease shrinkage" and "Increase shrinkage" buttons

The "Decrease indent" =F button and the "Increase indent" button are located in the "Paragraph" group.

Indentation values depend on the position of the tab stops (see section 4 below), which are set every 1.25 cm by default.

d) *Spacing and line spacing*

The *"Paragraph" window* can also be used to define :

- Precise *spacing between* selected *paragraphs* ;
- If you choose a spacing before and after, they will be added together.
- *Line spacing*, with line spacing defining the space *between lines*.

e) *The 4 types of alignment: left, centre, right and justify*

Alignments are made in relation to recesses if they exist, otherwise in relation to the left and right margins.

Use the 4 alignment buttons **to the left**, **centre= , right** and **justify**.

located in the Paragraph group, under the Home tab. The "Justify" mode stretches text from indent to indent, or from margin to margin.

f) *Line break in the same paragraph*

When you press Enter, a line break occurs (the cursor moves to the next line) and a new paragraph is created.

You can make a line break while remaining in the same paragraph: instead of typing Enter, type Shift + Enter.

"-l <

The character , is displayed at the end of the line when the "Show all" button is activated.

CHAPTER IV

INSERTING A WORD ART DOCUMENT

To insert a WordArt document, simply select the **Insert** menu> **Word Art**, then select the desired option.

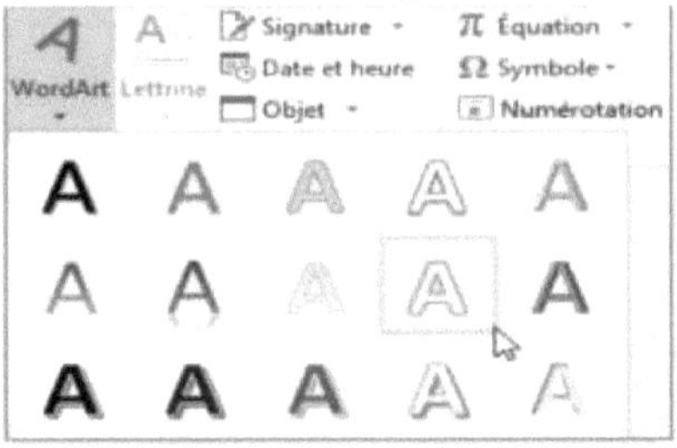

Enter your text

Transforming existing text into a WordArt object

1. Select the text.
2. Select **WordArt**, then the desired option.

Customise your WordArt object

1. Select the Word Art object.
2. Select **Text fill**, then choose an option.

CHAPTER V

PRINTING A DOCUMENT

1. To do this, select File > **Print**.
2. To preview each page, select the forward and back arrows at the bottom of the page
3. Choose the number of copies and other options, then select the Print button.

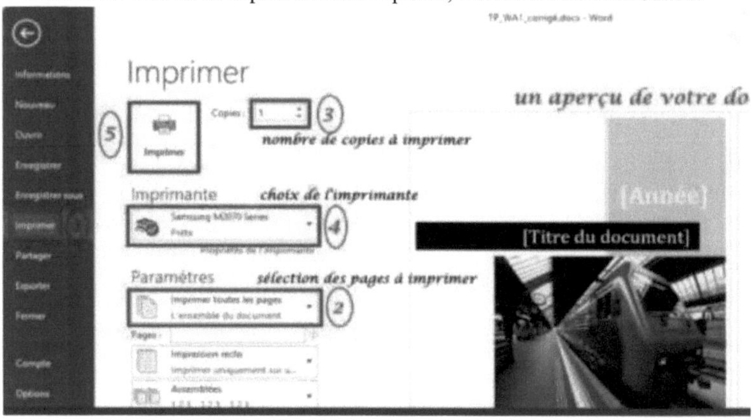

CHAPTER VI

PRACTICE

CHAPTER VII

INTRODUCTION TO EXCEL

VII.1. STARTING EXCEL

Cfr the same process as MS WORD

VII.2. CLOSING EXCEL

Just as it is possible to save all open documents at once in Word or Excel, it is also possible to close them all.

When you have finished adding and editing text in an Excel workbook, you should close the workbook to reduce desktop clutter. If the workbook is very large or contains a lot of images, closing the file also frees up memory and other system resources.

When you close a workbook, Excel automatically checks whether you have made any changes to the workbook since you last saved it. If Excel determines that the workbook contains unsaved changes, it prompts you to save the file. To avoid losing your work, be sure to save the workbook.

1) Display the workbook you wish to close.

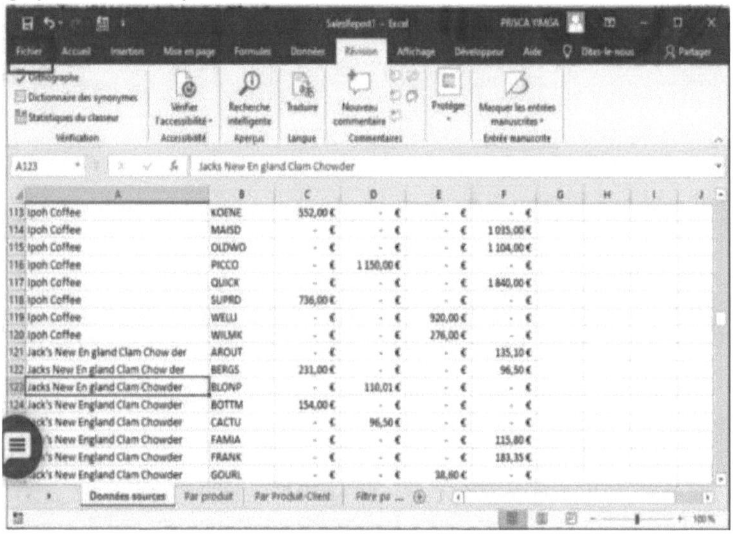

2) Click on the File tab.

V II.3.DIFFERENT EXCEL APPLICATION ZONES

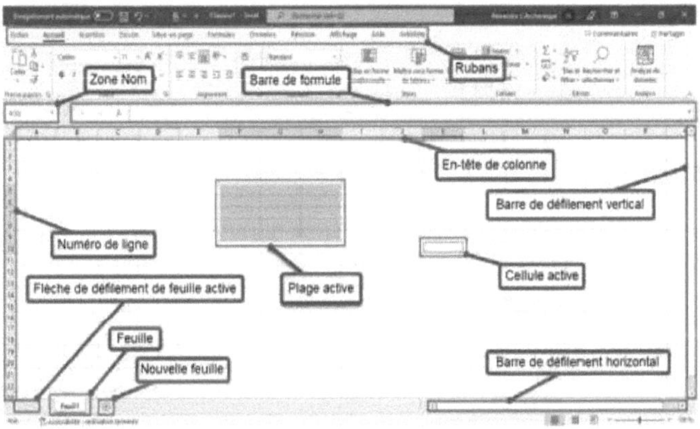

Name zone: Displays the name of the selected cell. It can also be used to name a range of cells with a specific name without spaces or special characters.
Formula bar: Displays formulas and functions for the active cell.
Line header: When we click on the line header (number), we select the entire line.
Active sheet scroll arrow: scrolls sheets to the right or left, which is very useful for large workbooks containing several sheets.
Sheet: Each sheet has 1,048,576 rows and 16,384 columns
Add sheet: Adds a sheet to the right of the selected sheet.
Ribbons: There are several ribbons that bring together a wide range of tools.
Active cell: Each cell on a sheet can contain a maximum of 32,767 characters.
Column header: When we click on the header (the letter) of a column, we select all the cells in the column simultaneously.
Vertical scroll bar: The vertical scroll bar is used to scroll the content of the displayed zone down or up when the height of the zone is insufficient to display its entire content.
Active range: This is the area that is greyed out when we select several adjacent cells so that we can manipulate them all at once.

Horizontal scroll bar: The horizontal scroll bar is used to scroll the content of the displayed area to the right or left when the width of the area is insufficient to display its entire content.

V II.4. TITLE BAR

The title bar **displays the name of the current workbook**. This area gives you one-click access to the commands you often use. This area gives you access to all of Excel's commands, options and features.

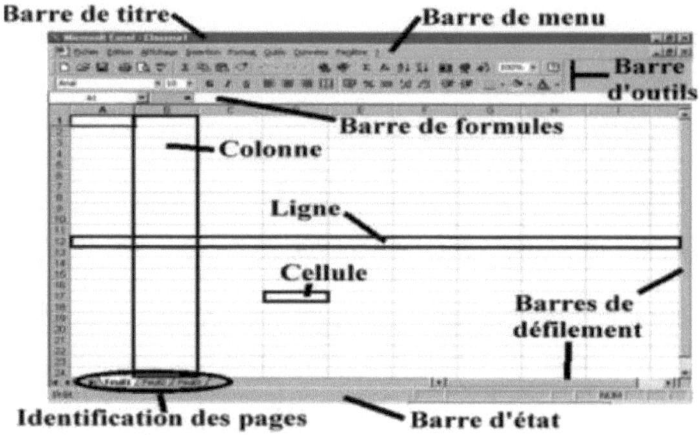

VII.5.DESCRIPTION OF THE EXCEL RIBBON

The Ribbon **is a set of toolbars located at the top of the interface. It gives you quick access to the various commands you might need in Excel**. It contains the main commands by default, but can be completely customized.
if necessary.

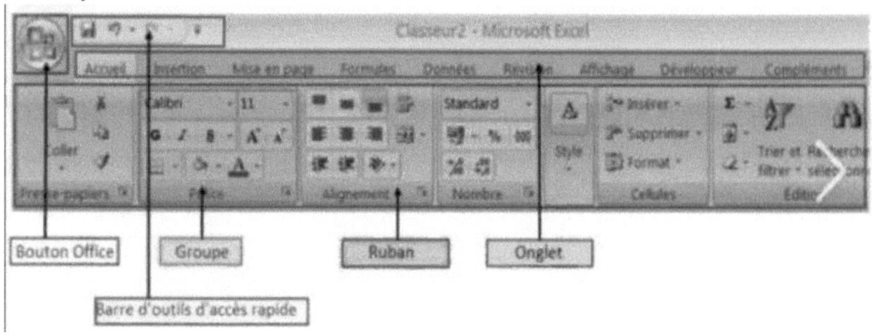

VII.6. CREATING A SIMPLE TABLE WITH EXCEL

V II.6.1. INSERTING AND DELETING ROWS AND COLUMNS

To insert or delete rows and columns in an Excel table, you can **:**

I- Select a cell in the column, then go to Home > Insert > Insert columns into the worksheet or Delete columns from the worksheet. You
Alternatively, right-click at the top of the column and select Insert or Delete to add or remove a column.

I- Select any cell in the table, right-click and go to "Insert". Select "Columns in the table on the left" or "Rows in the table above" from the pop-up menu to add one or the other.

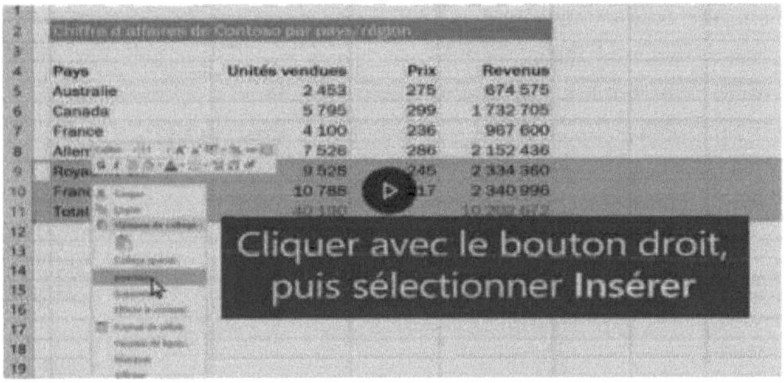

VII.6.2. NAMING A SHEET

1. Double-click on the **sheet** tab, then type in the new name.
2. Right-click on the **sheet** tab, click **Rename**, then type the new name.
3. Use the keyboard shortcut Alt+H > O > R then type the new name.

VII.6.3. WORKING WITH DIMENSIONS

To determine the default font for your spreadsheet, proceed as follows: 1. In the Format menu, click Style.
2. Read the font listed next to the Font checkbox.

To change the default font, proceed as follows:

1. In the Format menu, click Style.
2. Click on Modify.
3. On the Font tab, select the desired font, style and size.
4. Click on OK.

To change the default font in Excel 2007, proceed as follows :

1. On the **Page Setup** tab, in the **Themes** group, click **Fonts**.
2. Click **Create new theme fonts**.
3. In the **Title font** and **Body font** zones, select the fonts you want to use.
4. In the **Named** field, type **Office** to replace the default model.
5. Click on **Save**.

If the default font is a non-proportional font (fixed width), such as Courier, 8.43 characters of any type (numbers or letters) fit into a cell with a column width of 8.43, because all Courier characters have the same width. If the font is a proportional font, such as Arial, 8.43 integers (numbers such as 0, 1, 2, etc.) fit into a cell with a column width of 8.43. This is due to the fact that numbers are spaced with most proportional fonts. However, letters are not spaced with proportional fonts, more "i" characters fit and fewer "w" characters.

When you replace the width of a column with a fractional number, the column width can be set to a different number depending on the font used in the Normal style. For example, with a Normal style font of Arial, if you try to change the width of a column to 8.5, the column is set 8.57 or 65 pixels. This behaviour occurs because of the translation of font characters into pixel units. Fractional pixel units cannot be displayed, so the column width is rounded to the nearest number, resulting in a whole pixel unit.

Example of column width behaviour

1. In a new Excel workbook, select cell A1.
2. In the Format menu, point to Column, then click Width.
3. In the Column **width** field, type 10 (75 pixels wide), then click OK.
4. In the Format menu, click on Style, then check that the default font is correctly set to Arial 10.
5. In cell A1, type 1234567890.

NB: The letters fit perfectly into the cell and the column width is always 10 (75 pixels wide).

6. In the Format menu, click Style.
7. Click on Modify.
8. On the Font tab, replace the font with Courier New, then double-click OK. Note that the Column Width field automatically updates to support the new font and that the number in the cell is still appropriate, even though the column width is still 10, but has increased to 85 pixels wide.

Column width behaviour in Excel 2007

To set the column width in Excel 2007, proceed as follows :

1. In the first column, click **A** to select the column, then right-click and select **Column width**.
2. Enter the desired width for your column.
3. Click **OK**.

The behaviour of column width in Excel 2007 is the same as that shown above. If you change the fonts after defining the width, the width is adjusted to the new width of the font pixels.

VII.6.4. FORMATTING A TABLE

Excel offers a number of predefined table styles that you can use to format a table in the blink of an eye. If the predefined table styles don't suit you, you can create and apply a custom table style. Although you can only delete custom table styles, you can remove a predefined table style so that it is no longer applied to a table.

	A	B	C	D
1	Produit	Tri 1	Tri 2	Total génér
2	Chocolade	744,60 €	162,56 €	907,16 €
3	Gummibarchen	5 079,60 €	1 249,20 €	6 328,80 €
4	Longbreads écossais	1 267,50 €	1 062,50 €	2 330,00 €
5	Scones Sir Rodney	1 418,00 €	756,00 €	2 174,00 €
6	Tarte au sucre	4 728,00 €	4 547,92 €	9 275,92 €
7	Biscuits au chocolat	943,89 €	349,60 €	1 293,49 €
8	Total	14 181,59 €	8 127,78 €	22 309,37 €

You can also adjust the layout of the table by choosing the quick style options corresponding to elements of the table, for example **Header row**, **Total row**, **First column**, **Last column**, **Striped rows** and **Striped columns** or **Filter button.**

VII.6.5. STYLE CHOICE

CHOOSE A TABLE STYLE

When a range of data is not formatted as a table, Excel automatically converts it to a table when you select a table style. You can also change the layout of an existing table by selecting another layout.

1. Select the table cell or range of cells to which you want to apply table formatting.

2. On the **Home** tab, click **Set as table**.

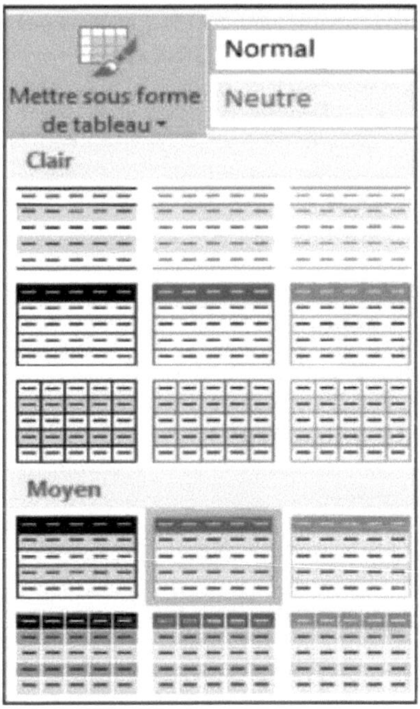

Note:

- **Auto preview**: Excel automatically formats your table or data range with the preview style you select, but only applies that style if you press Enter or click the mouse to confirm your choice. You can browse table layouts using the mouse or the arrow keys on your keyboard.
- When you use the **Set as table** option, Excel automatically converts your data range into a table. If you no longer wish to manipulate your data in a table, you can convert it back into a conventional range, while retaining the formatting you have applied.

VII.6.6. ALIGNMENTD IN CELLS

If you want to realign the text in a cell to improve the visual presentation of your data, here's how to do it:

1. Select the cells containing the text you want to align.
2. In the **Home** tab, choose one of the following alignment options:

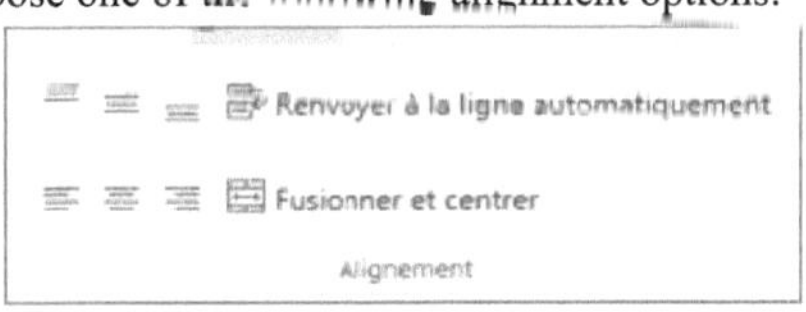

3. **To align the text vertically, choose Align top , Align centre or Align bottom** .
4. To align text horizontally, choose **Align text left , centre** or align text right .
5. When you a long line of text, part of the text may not be visible. To solve this problem

without changing the column width, click Return to **line automatically**.

6. To centre text that spans several columns or rows, click on **merge & centre**.

VII.6.7. CENTRING ON SEVERAL COLUMNS

You can make a spreadsheet more attractive and easier to read by centring text across several columns. Often you do this by merging and centring the merged cells, but that's not the only option.

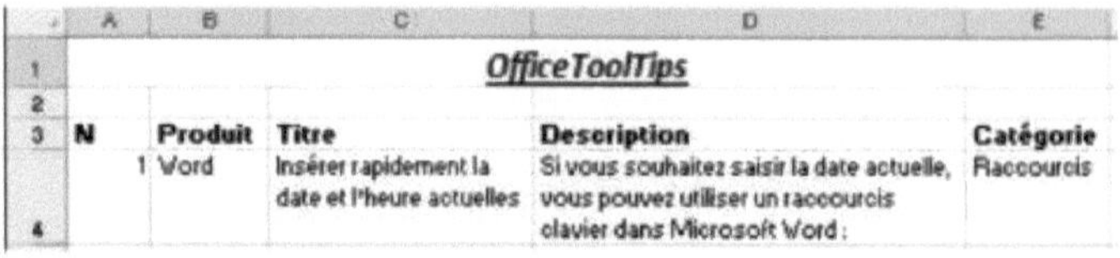

To centre text across several columns, proceed as follows :

1. Select a range made up of the text and cells you want to centre on this text :

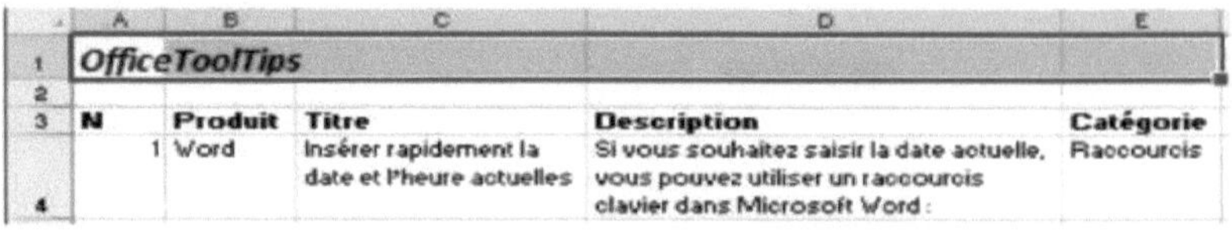

2. On the **Home** tab, in the **Alignment** group, click the launcher arrow for the dialog box :

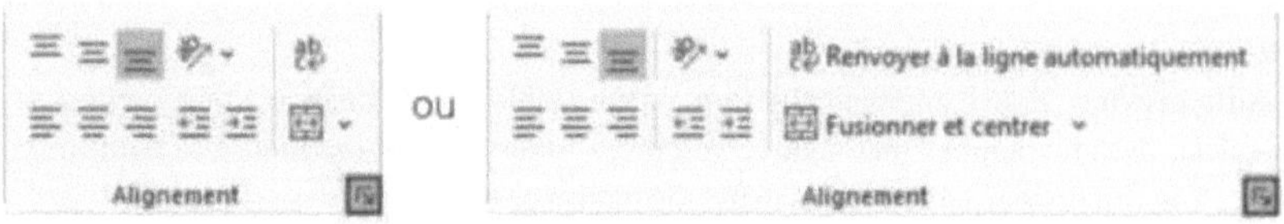

3. In the **Format cell** dialogue box, under the **Alignment** tab, click on the list **Horizontal**, then select **Centred on several columns** :

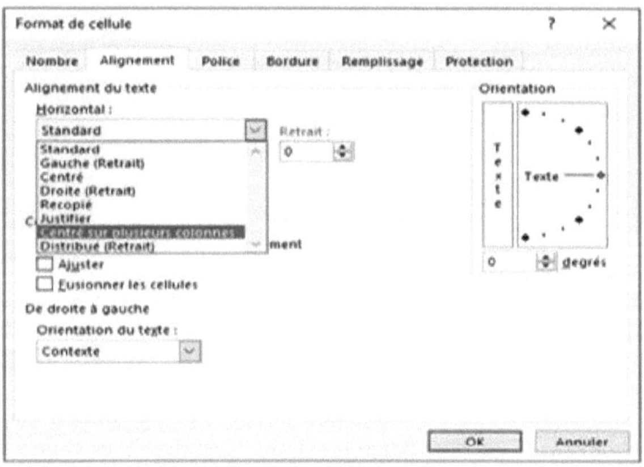

4. Click **OK**.

VII.6.8. TEXT FORMATTING

Formatting text or numbers can make them more visible, especially when you have a large worksheet. Changing default formats includes things like changing the font colour, style, size, alignment of text in a cell, or applying formatting effects.

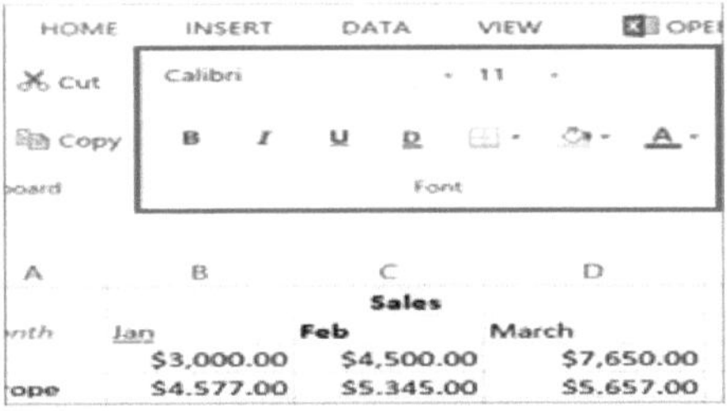

If you want the text or numbers in a cell to appear bold, italicised, single-underlined or double-underlined, select the cell and, on **the Home tab,** choose the format you want:

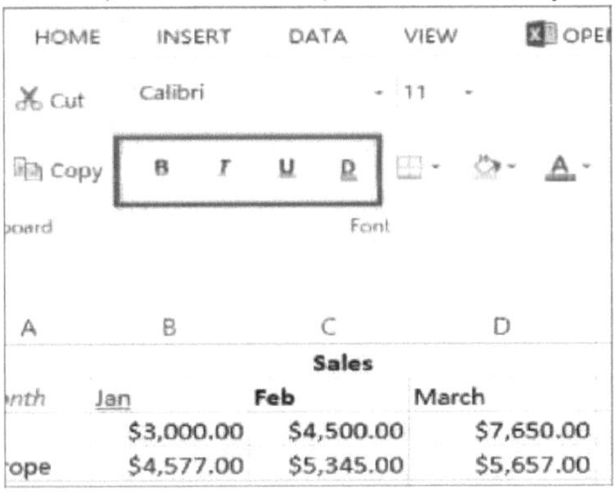

1. **Change font style, size, colour or apply effects**

Click on **Home** and:

-1- For a different font style, click on the arrow next to the **default Calibri** font and choose the style you want.

-2- To increase or decrease the font size, click on the arrow next to the default size 11 and choose another text size.

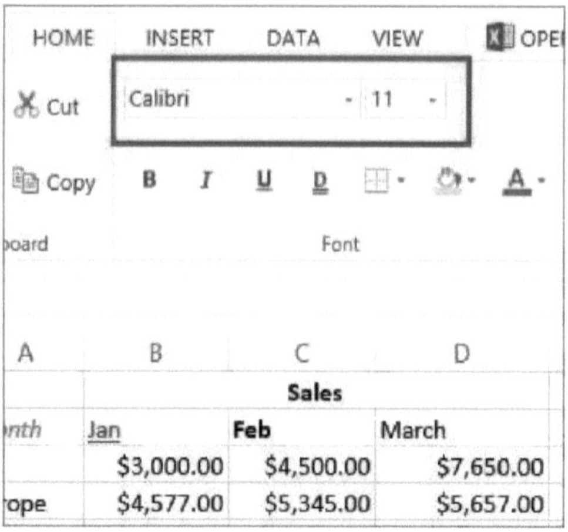

-3- To change the font colour, click **on Font Colour** and choose a colour.
-4- To add a background colour, click on **Fill colour** next to font **colour.**

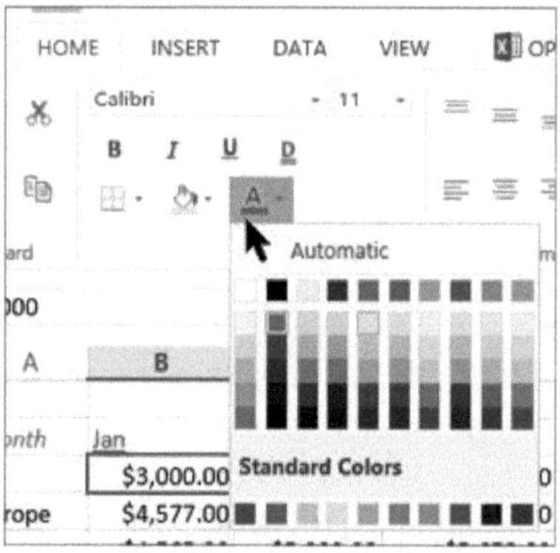

-5- To apply strikethrough, superscript or subscript formatting, click on the Launcher dialogue box, and select an option under **Effects**.

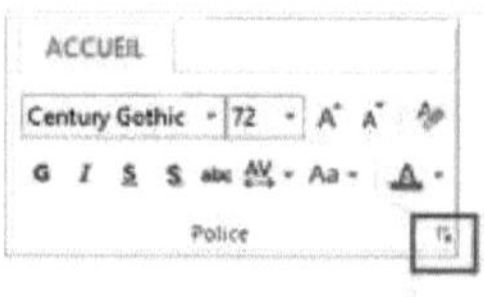

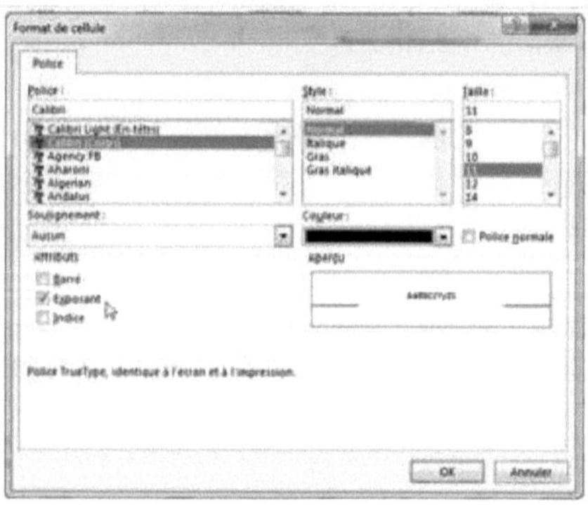

2. Change text alignment

You can position the text in a cell so it is centred, left-aligned or right-aligned. If it is a long line of text, you can **apply wrap text** so that all the text is visible.

Select the text you want to align, and on the **Home** tab, choose alignment option you want.

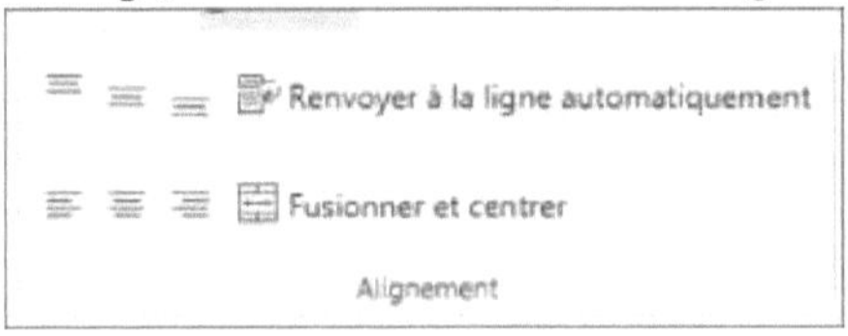

3. Delete formatting

If you change your mind after applying any formatting, to undo it, select the text and on **the Home tab,** click **Clear>** .

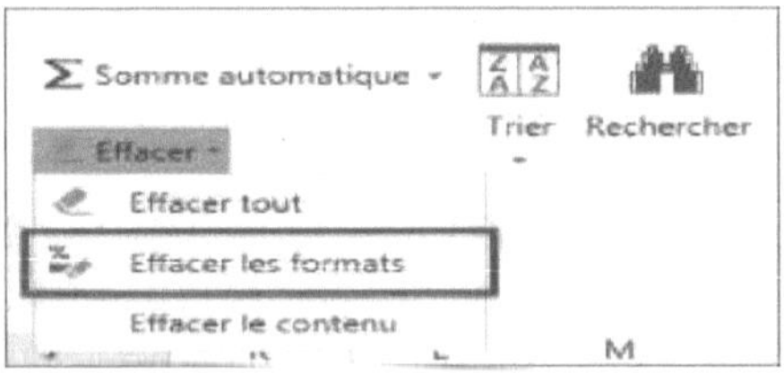

VII.6.9.APPLICATION OF REASONS

In Excel, we all know the basic function for applying a background colour to one or more Excel cells.

This is represented by the following icon in the Home tab and positioned in the Font section.

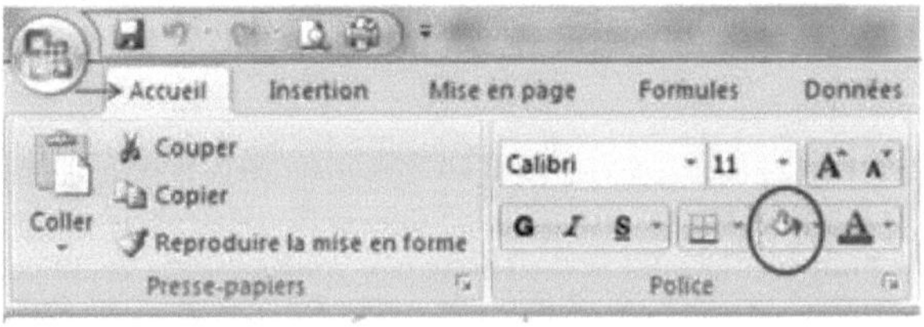

To personalise our cells a little more, we can also apply a pattern to them, and we'll see how here.

If you try to go through the Fill colour icon above, you can see that even when you click on the drop-down arrow and select Other colours, whether in the Standard or Custom tabs, you are not able to choose a pattern.

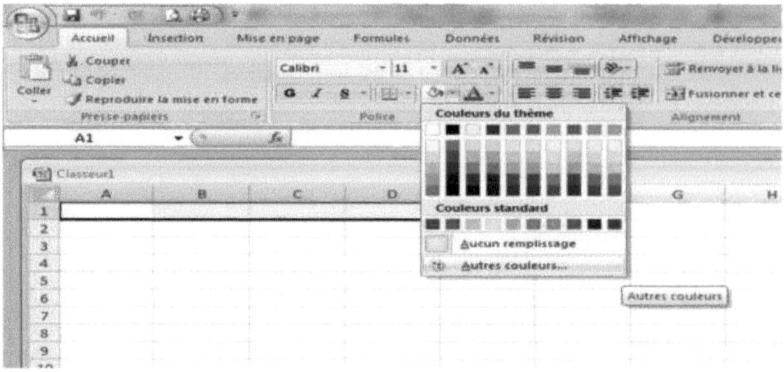

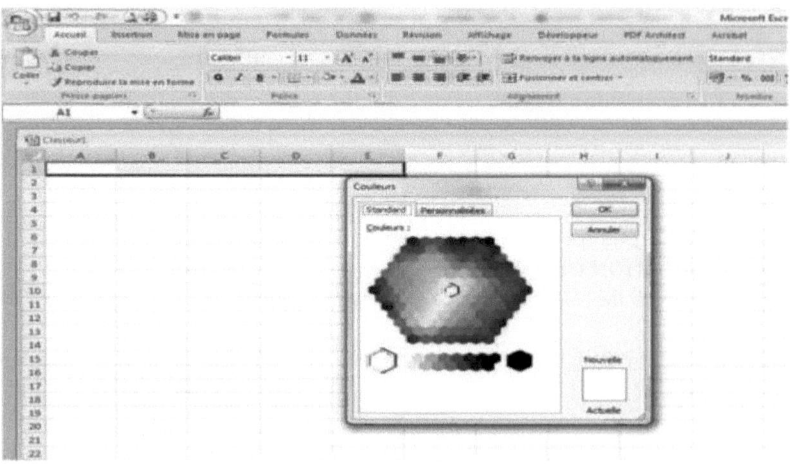

To apply a pattern to your cell, you will need to use Excel's "hidden" functions.

To do this, in the **Font** section, still in the **Home** tab**,** you can see a small icon at the bottom right of this section, represented by a small arrow in a "half-square".

By clicking on this icon, you can access all the functions in this section, which concern all cell formats.

Tip: to save time, you can also access it using the shortcut :

Ctrl + Shift + F.

VII.6.10. LAYOUT AND PRINTING

Excel you print out your document and add to its presentation. You can add a header or footer, change the margins, add or omit workbook rows and much more.

PAGE LAYOUT

The page layout options are there to improve the presentation of your workbook on paper. You can change sheet margins, title displays and many other options, which will be described below.

1. From the **File** menu, select the **Page Setup** option.

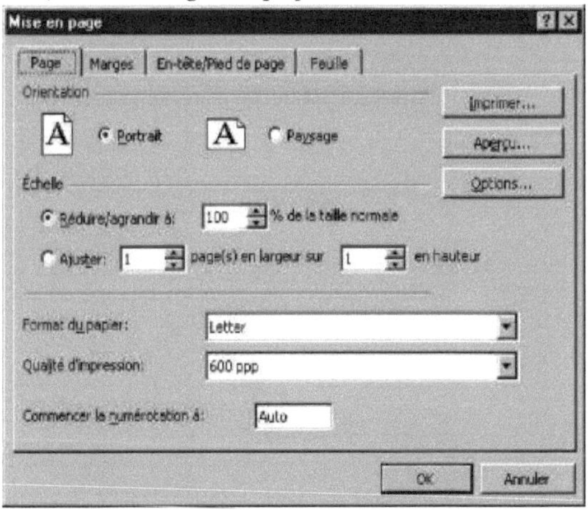

2. Under the page tab, there are options for presenting the workbook on paper. In the first block, Excel asks you for the orientation of the pages to be printed. The second block asks you at what scale to print your workbook. This becomes important when one of the columns in your document prints on the next page instead of the page you would have liked. You can change the scale manually to reduce or increase the scale of the text. You can also ask Excel to automatically find the right scale for entering your document X pages wide and Y pages high. You can view the print preview at any time. You can also change the type of paper (letter, legal, tabloid, etc.) and the print quality. For printing in computer , make sure that the paper size is always "US Letter". The last option allows you to choose the page number at which printing will start. For example, the first page of your printout could be numbered page 5 and so on.

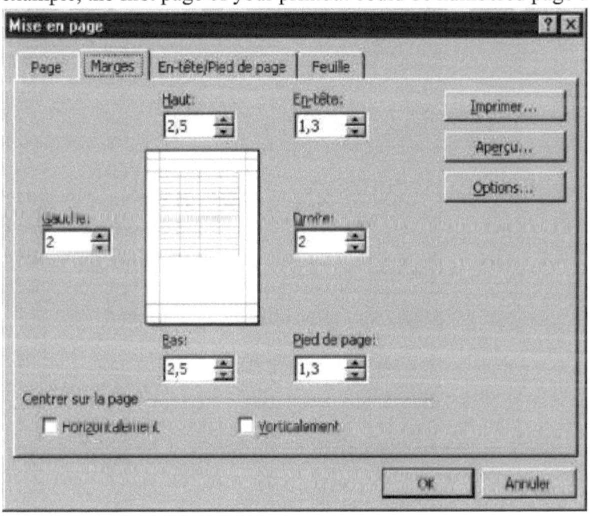

3. On the Margins tab, you can set the margins for the workbook and for the header and footer. You can also choose to centre your worksheet horizontally and vertically on the page. You can also determine the location for the document header and footer. The preview in the middle of the window gives you an idea of the effect of these choices on the paper.

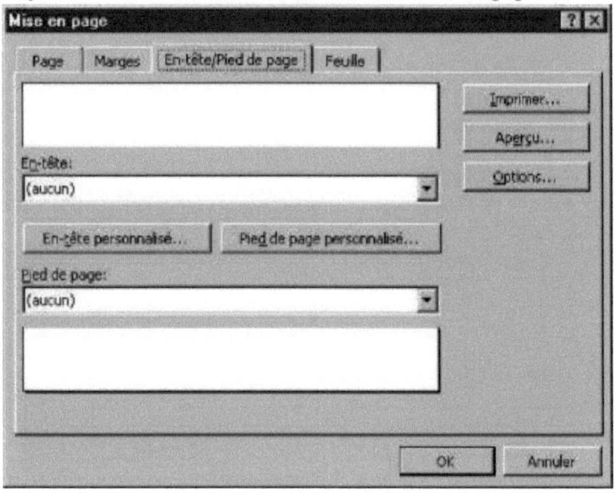

4. Under the Header/Footer tab, you determine what will be displayed in the header and footer of each page of the printout. If you don't want a header or footer, select the "(none)" option, which is the first on the list of predetermined items.

CUSTOMISE THE HEADER AND FOOTER.

5. Press the Custom header button.

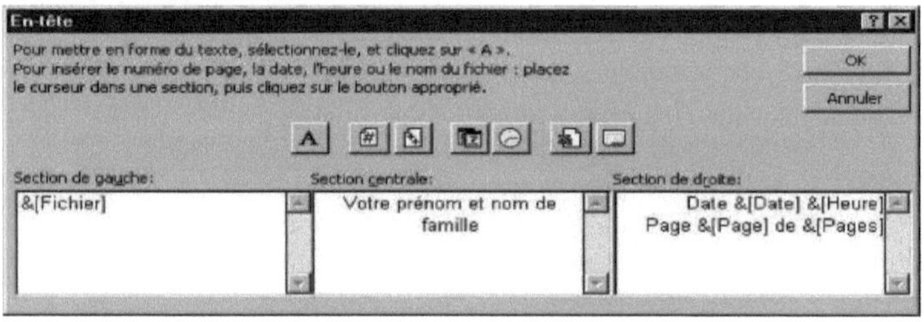

The options for customising the header when printing appear above. There are the same options for the footer. The top part of the window has a series of buttons with the most frequently used options. The bottom section is divided into three boxes. The left-hand box contains the text that will be pasted into the left-hand margin of the page. The middle box contains the text that will be pasted in the middle of the header and so on.click in the left-hand box.

a. Press the _ button to insert the file name.

b. Click in the middle box.

c. Write your **first** and **last name**.

d. Click in the box on the right.

e. Write: **Date:** and press the et

f. Press Enter.

g. Write **Page** and press the .

h. Write **de** and press the 

i. Press the **OK** button.

j. Press the **Preview** button

k. Press the zoom button to see the header more clearly.

The result should look like this.

Class1 Votre prénom et nom de famille Date 23/09/95 09:49
Page 1 de 1

Classi Your first and last name Date23fl9/95 09:49
Page 1 of 1

This last exercise demonstrated that you can use the option buttons, write text or combine the two to give a better result. It is also possible to have several lines in the header.

l. Press the **Close** button to return to the page layout options.

m. Click on **the Sheet** tab.

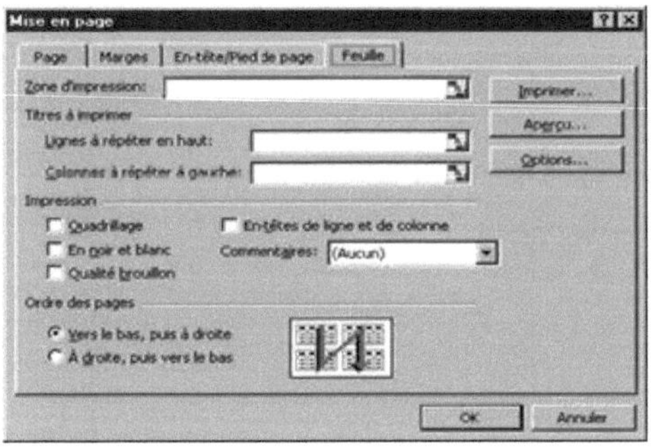

In the Sheet tab, you can specify which block will be printed in the print area box. You can determine how much of your spreadsheet will be printed. Instead of printing the entire contents a spreadsheet, you can choose print only part of it.

The title boxes are very practical. We often use the first rows and columns of a spreadsheet to write important headings such : income, expenses, gross profit, net profit, a list of months, a list of important items or accounts, etc. But these headings will not be reprinted on the second and subsequent pages unless Excel is forced to do so. But these headings will not be reprinted on the second and subsequent pages unless you force Excel to do so.

You need to indicate which rows and columns you want to print on each page of your printout. Be careful not to put these rows and columns in the print area. Otherwise, they print twice on the first page of your printout.

CHAPTER VIII

WORD DOCUMENT PROCESSING

VIII.1. OPERATIONS ON TABLES, FONTS AND PARAGRAPHS

VIII.1.1. MODIFICATION OF THE POLICY

When you create a new blank document in Word, any text you type appears in the default font, called **Calibri**, with a font size of **11** points, which is a standard size for text in Word documents (such as letters or reports).

If you prefer to use another font or size as standard for your documents, change it as follows :

1. Create a new empty document.
2. Type a short example sentence, then select it. This text will give you a better idea of the font:
3. Right-click on the selection, then choose **Font...** from the context menu (or press **Ctrl+D**) to open the **Font** dialog box:

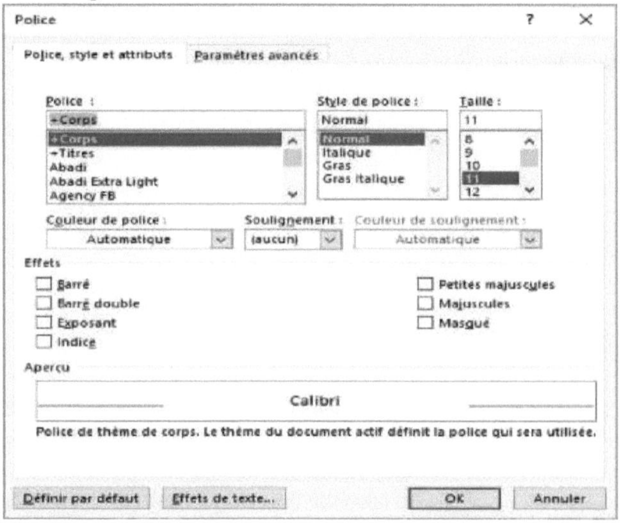

4. Choose the font, font style, font size, colour, underlining and any other effects. Look at the **Preview** area to see what your sample text looks like with your choices.
5. Click on the **Set as default** button.

Word displays the confirmation dialog box as follows:

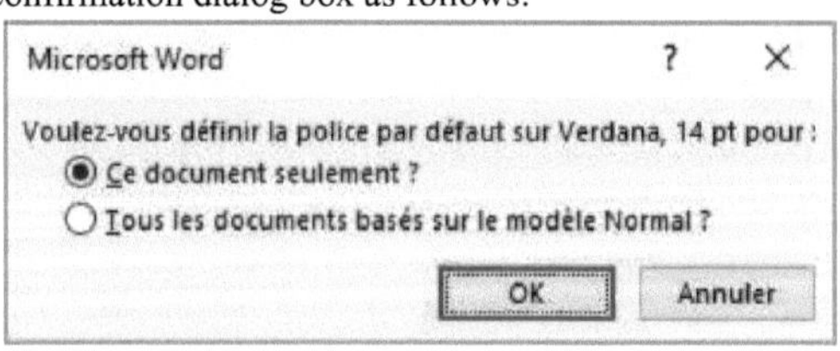

Note: Word does not modify documents you have already created.

VIII.1.2. CHANGING THE SPACING BETWEEN CHARACTERS

Selecting **Extended** or **Condensed** changes the spacing between all the selected letters based on a common value. Kerning changes the spacing between specific pairs of letters; sometimes decreasing it, sometimes increasing it, depending on the letters.

A. Expand or condense the space evenly between all the selected characters

1. Select the text you want to change.
2. Under the **Home** tab, click on the **Font** ' ^ dialogue box launcher (circled in green in the screenshot below), then click on the **Advanced** tab .

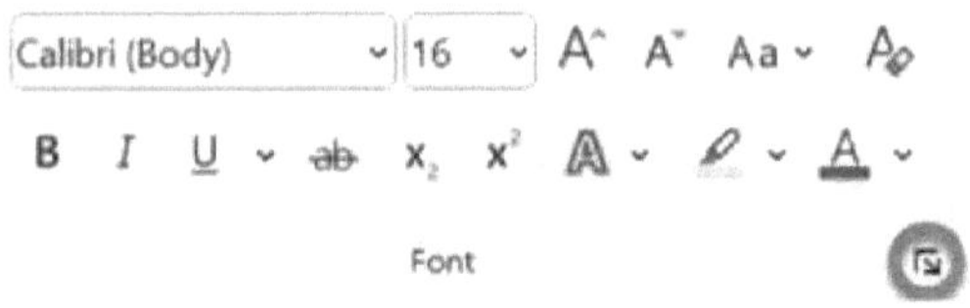

3. In the **Spacing** area, click **Extended** or **Condensed**, then specify the amount of space you want in the **From** area.

B. Create characters larger than a specific size

Kerning refers to the way in which the spacing between two specific characters is adjusted. The idea is to achieve a better result by reducing the spacing between characters that fit together well (such as 'A' and 'V') and increasing the spacing between characters that do not.

1. Select the text you want to change.
2. Under the **Home** tab, click on the **Font** ' ^ dialogue box launcher (circled in green in the screenshot below), then click on the **Advanced** tab.

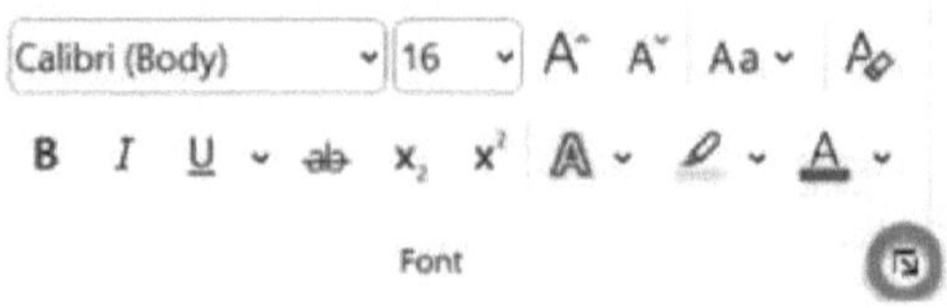

3. Tick the **Kerning** box, then enter the size in points in the **points and over** field.

C. Stretch or scale text horizontally

When you scale text, you change the shapes of the characters by a defined percentage. You can scale text by stretching or compressing it.

1. Select the text you want to stretch or compress.
2. Under the **Home** tab, click on the **Font ' ^** dialogue box launcher (circled in green in the screenshot below), then click on the **Advanced** tab.

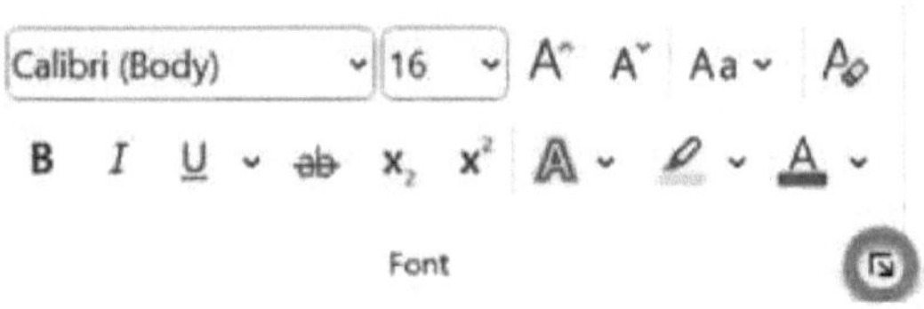

3. In the **Scale** box, enter the desired percentage.

Text is stretched with percentages above 100%. Text is compressed with percentages below 100%.

D. Changing the line spacing

The best way to increase or decrease the amount of vertical space between lines of text in a paragraph is to change the style used by the paragraph.

1. Find the style you are using in the **Styles** gallery under the **Home** tab.
2. Right-click on the style to be modified and select **Modify**.

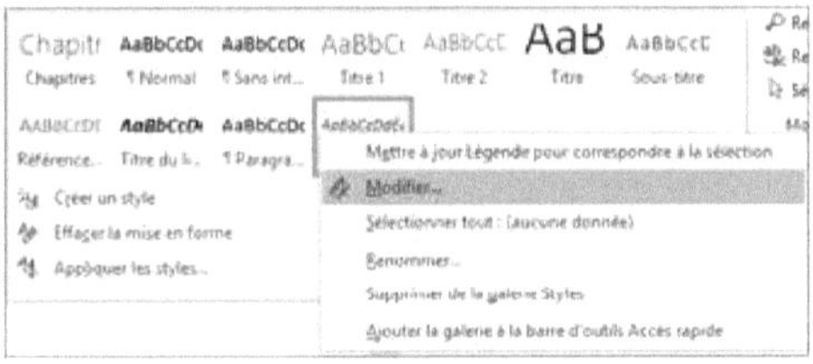

3. Near the centre of the dialogue box are the line spacing buttons, which allow you to select single, 1.5x or double line spacing. Select the spacing you want to apply, then click **OK**.

If you want to apply a more specific line spacing to the style, click the **Format** button in the bottom left-hand corner of the **Edit Style** dialog box, then select **Paragraph**. The Line **spacing** drop-down list allows you to select or set a more specific line spacing.

VIII.1.3. INDENTATIONS, SPACING AND LINE SPACING

On the Home tab, select Line and paragraph **spacing** > **Line spacing** options. The Paragraph dialog box opens. On the **Indents** and **Spacing** tab, select the desired options, then click OK.

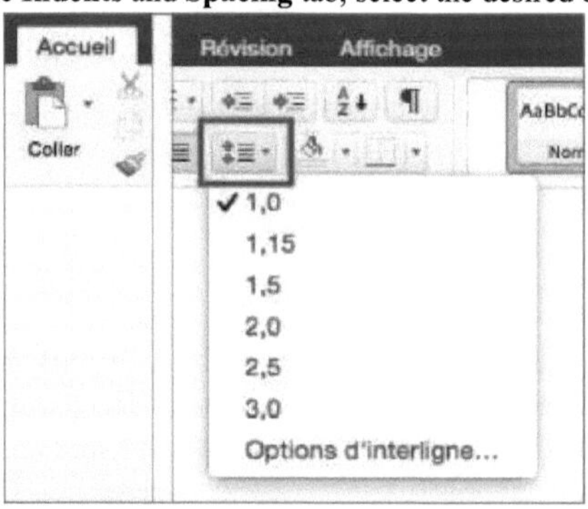

VIII.2. INSERTION OF A COVER PAGE

The cover page reflects the image and content of a document and invites the reader to enter. With Word 2010, you can easily add predefined cover pages to your documents.

1. Open **Insertions** tab of the Ribbon.

2. In the **Pages** section, click **Cover page**.

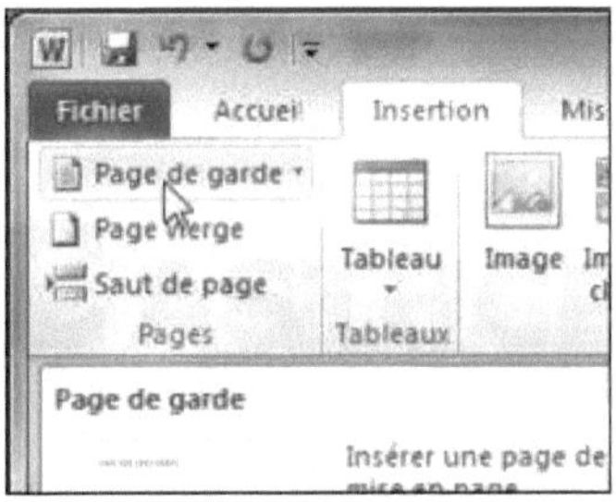

3. Click on a predefined cover page in the gallery that appears.

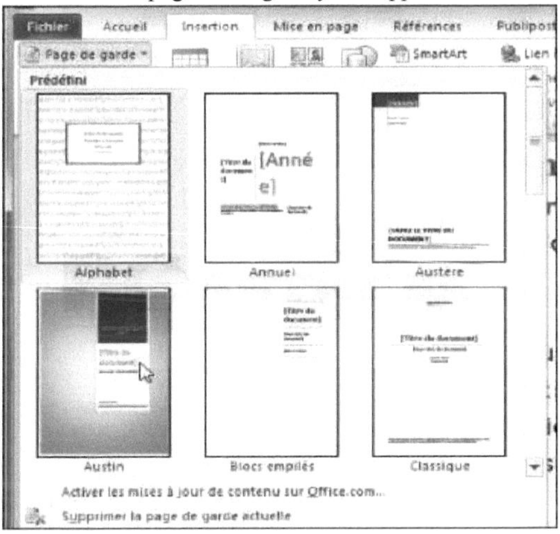

4. Click on the various elements of the cover page (title, date, etc.) to remove them. personalise.

VIII.3. INSERTING TEXT INTO A TEXT IN A DOCUMENT EXISTING

To insert a Word document into another Word document, follow the steps below.

1. First open the document that will be used to support the existing file.
2. Make sure your cursor is where the file will go.
3. Go to "Insert > Text > Object > Text from file".

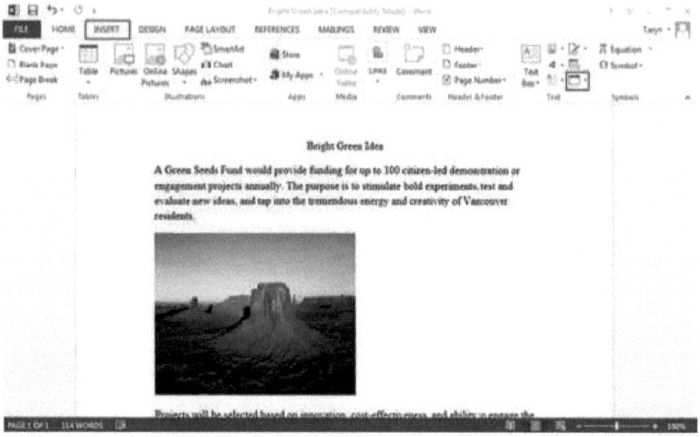

1. Find and select the file you want to insert.
2. Then double-click on the file to import your file.

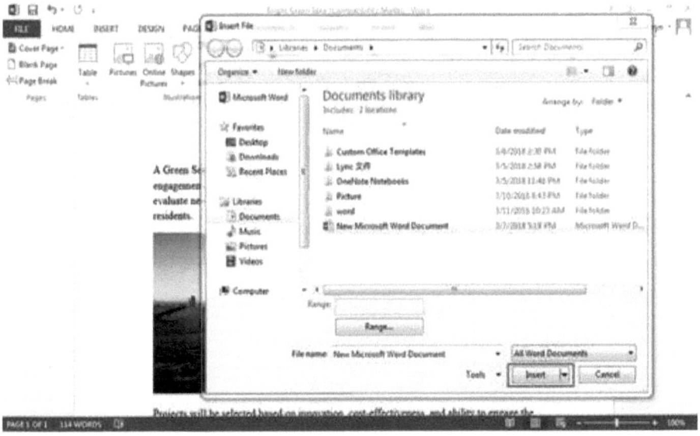

It is important to note that some of the highlighted steps for inserting a Word document into another Word document may vary depending on the version of Word you are using. However, they are almost the same, with just a few minor variations, especially for new versions of Word, but there's nothing to worry about.

VIII.4. INSERTING A PAGE BREAK

1. Place the **cursor** at the exact point where you want to insert the page break.

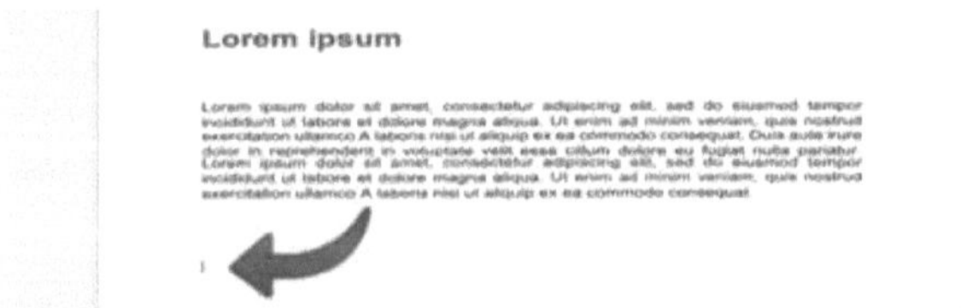

2. Click on the **Page Setup** tab (or Layout tab on versions of Word plus). Anciennes).

3. Click on **Page break** (or Break on older versions of Word) ;

4. Click on **Page** ;

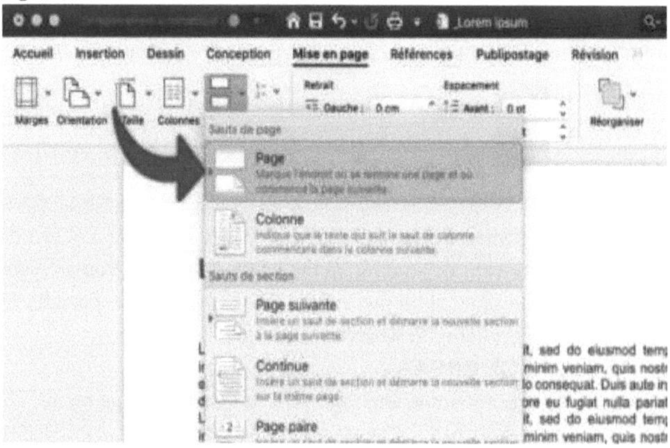

Want to delete a page break? No problem. First, click on the **Home** tab and then on the **Show formatting marks** button. This brings up the page breaks, among others. Select the one you want to delete and press the **Delete** key on your keyboard.

VIII.5. INSERTING A LINE USING THE CONTEXT MENU

Alternatively, you can use the context menu (accessible by right-clicking), after selecting a row in the table. Choose the Insert rows option to add a row between the one you have selected and the one above it.

CHAPTER IX

DEFINITION OF BASIC COMPUTING CONCEPTS

IX.1. DATA

Conventional representation of information for automatic processing.

IX.2. INFORMATION

In computing and telecommunications, information is an element of knowledge (voice, data, image) that can be stored, processed or transmitted using a standardised medium and coding method .[12]

IX.3. AUTOMATIC PROCESSING

A series of operations performed on data by a computer to retrieve, transform or classify information .[13]

IX.4. COMPUTER

Automatic information processing machine, obeying programmes formed by sequences of arithmetic and logical operations.

IX.5. PROGRAMME :

A list instructions telling a computer what to do. It the form of one or more sequences of instructions, often including basic data, to be executed in a certain order by a processor or by a computer process (in the case of multitasking systems) .[14]

IX.6. SOFTWARE

An **application** is a set of programs that enables a computer or computer system to perform a particular task or function (e.g. customer relationship management software, production software, accounting software, loan management software) .[15]

IX.7. COMPUTER LANGUAGE

A language designed to describe the set of consecutive actions that a computer must perform. A computer language is therefore a practical way for us (humans) to give instructions to a computer .[16]

IX.8. MICRO-COMPUTING

Computer technology relating to the manufacture and use of microcomputers .[17]

IX.9. COMPUTER VIRUSES

A virus is a malicious computer program designed to disrupt the normal operation of a computer system without the owner's knowledge .[18]

IX.10. COMPUTER ANTI-VIRUS

An antivirus is a computer program designed to identify and delete malicious software (*malware*), also known as viruses, Trojan horses or worms, depending on the form .[19]

---

[12] https://www.toupie.org/Dictionnaire/Information.htm , consulted on 27/09/2023 at 00:27

[13] https://langue-francaise.tv5monde.com, consulted on 27/09/2023 at 00:28 a.m.

[14] https://www.techno-science.net, consulted on 27/09/2023 at 00:34 a.m.

[15] Idem, consulted on 27/09/2023 at 00:37 a.m.

[16] https://web.maths.unsw.edu.au, consulted on 27/09/2023 at 00:40

[17] Ibidem, consulted on 27/09/2023 at 00:43 a.m.

[18] https://www.cybermalveillance.gouv.fr, consulted on 27/09/2023 at 00:45'.

[19] https://www.futura-sciences.com, consulted on 27/09/2023 at 00:49 am

IX.11. FILES

An organised collection of information, designated by a precise name, which the operating system of a computer manipulates as a single entity, in its memory or on a storage medium .[20]

[20] https://www.larousse.fr, consulted on 27/09/2023 at 00:51 a.m.

CHAPTER X

COMPUTER

X.1.TYPES OF COMPUTER

Computers are becoming an increasingly essential part of our daily lives. They make life easier for businesses and individuals in all sectors.

However, the fact that there are so many different models creates a major confusion in the minds of consumers. Most of the time, it's hard to decide which type is best suited to your needs and usage. In this article, we take a look at the different computers available on the market.

A. DESKTOP COMPUTERS

So-called desktop computers are designed for on-site use. Their heavy weight means that they cannot be transported easily and permanently. They are also powered by electricity.

As a result, they need to be installed close an electrical socket on a wooden or metal support in the home, office, etc. Consisting of a case, microprocessor, motherboard, processing memory, etc., they are designed exclusively for home or business use. Other important characteristics of desktop computers are :

- a screen;
- a keyboard ;
- With a mouse;
- a internal ;
- A loudspeaker...

B. LAPTOPS

The emphasis here is on practicality. As its name suggests, a laptop allows users to take it anywhere. Whether in the office, on the beach, at the cinema or at home, it works perfectly and can be used for a multitude of tasks. What's more, laptops are designed for all kinds of users: students, employees, teachers, etc. can all make effective use of them. It's packed with high-performance features, including :

- One screen ;
- Integrated **mouse** and keyboard,
- A Web Cam, etc.

What's more, the laptop is very light and easy to carry.

C. GAMER COMPUTERS[20]

It's a computer tool developed to satisfy the desires of computer game lovers. It is reputed to be a very powerful and durable computer. So it's a kind of stationary computer, complete with keyboard, motherboard, ergonomic mouse, pedals, etc. The gamer is a very important tool, because regular play on a conventional computer can damage it and shorten its lifespan.
For ease of use and longevity, each type of computer should be chosen with the consumer's needs in mind.

X.2. STRUCTURE AND OPERATION OF A BASIC COMPUTER SYSTEM

The term "computer" originally meant an electronic digital calculator. The French term "Ordinateur" seems more appropriate today, moving away from the digital connotation. The computer is now defined as a machine for processing information.
A computer is capable of acquiring and storing information, processing it and retrieving the information stored.

A) Definition: Computer system

[20] Idem, consulted on 27/09/2023 at 01:05 a.m.

A computer system is the set of software and hardware resources required to meet the user's computing needs.

B) General diagram of an IT system

At first glance, a computer is made up of :

- a processor which carries out the processing ;
- a central memory where this processor stores the data and results of these treatments ;
- peripherals exchanging information with the outside world.

All these components are linked together via buses, which are the central arteries and enable them to exchange data.

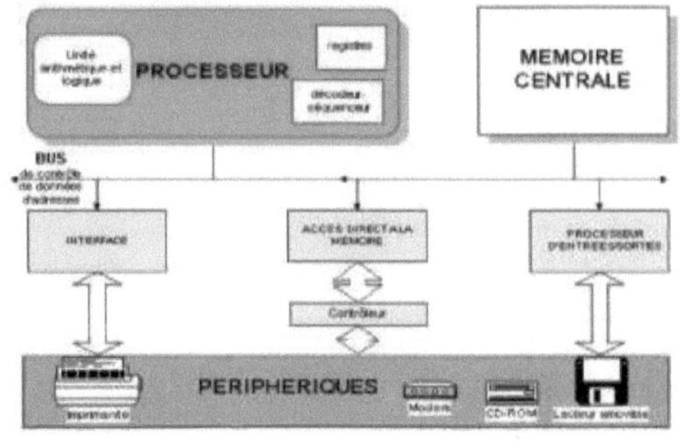

X.3. PARTS OF THE COMPUTER

X.3.1. HARDWARE

DEFINITION

Hardware is the material part of a computer. It is made up of all the hardware components, i.e. the visible parts of a computer. These components may be internal or external to the CPU. External components include the screen, keyboard and mouse. Internal components include the hard disk.

Etymology of hardware

Hardware is an Anglicism, a combination of "**hard**" and "ware". The term is attested in the mid-sixteenth century meaning metal material. In the sense of the hardware part of a computer, it is attested from 1947.(1)

Hardware composition

A computer's hardware is made up of visible and invisible components. Visible components are visible devices such as the central processing unit and peripherals. Invisible components are those located inside the central processing unit, such as the motherboard, microprocessor, memory, graphics card, sound card and storage media (hard disk, floppy drive, CD-ROM/DVD-ROM drives/writers).

Hardware is generally made up of the following elements:

1. a main unit (the box and its contents)
2. a monitor or screen
3. a keyboard
4. a mouse
5. input-output interfaces
6. external peripherals (printers, scanners, etc.)
7. internal peripherals (sound and video cards, etc.)
8. various readers, various expansion cards, etc.

X.3.2. SOFTWARE

Software is the term used to describe the immaterial, intelligent and virtual part of your machine. In French, the term simply means software, or even application or programme.

Software represents all the computer codes and essential programmes installed on your PC, which contribute to its smooth operation. In fact, it is thanks to the programme that it can carry out a digital task. For example, there is software designed for services such as management, which enables you to produce estimates and invoices in a specific format, software for accounting, software that enables you to monitor production and consult company's stock levels, and software that enables you to protect your confidential data.

Software is characterised by a sequence of instructions that must be interpreted and executed by your PC. Software can be classified into several categories:

- System software, better known as operating systems such as Windows or Linux
- The application
- Programming software

X.4. OPERATION OF A MICROCOMPUTER

X.4.1. BASIC CONCEPT

1) **Material structure Internal structure** :

- motherboard
- processor

RAM expansion cards (sound card, graphics card, internal modem, network card).

2) **External structure :**

- memory card readers (USB, MS, CompactFlash, SmartMedia, MMC/SD, etc.)
- mouse
- keyboard
- screen (monitor)
- combined DVD player (printer, photocopier, scanner)
- ADSL modem .

3) How it works PC = caterer of data digital

Analogue data (text, sound, images) 0 digital data (bits = signal with a succession of 0s and 1s which form a byte in a sequence of 8)

- 1 KB (Kilobyte = 103 bytes)
- 1 MB (Megabyte = 106 bytes)
- 1 GB (Gigabyte = 109 bytes)
- 1TB (Terabyte = 1012bytes)
- 1 KB = Kilobyte: 1 thousand bytes 0 one page of text
- 1 MB = Megabyte: 1 million0 a 400-page book
- 1 Go = Gigabyte: 1 billion 0 a bookshelf
- 1 To = Terabyte: bytes 0 an entire library

A) Processor in charge of data processing

Its processing speed corresponds to the clock frequency expressed in Gigahertz (GHz). Most processors are manufactured by Intel (Pentium) and AMD (Turion and Athlon). The clock frequency determines the computer's processing speed. It is now expressed in Gigahertz (GHz): the higher the clock frequency, the faster the PC. For example: in 2000, the Pentium 4 was launched in a 1400 Mhz version; today it reaches 3 Ghz, i.e. a frequency twice as fast. In Windows, the "System Properties" dialogue box displays the name of the processor and its clock frequency: Click on Start > Control Panel > System.

B) Motherboard

All the components connect to it (processor, expansion cards, RAM) The motherboard is a large printed circuit board on which a large number of electronic chips, sockets and other circuits are mounted. All the electronic components are connected to this board: the processor, the expansion cards (sound card, graphics card, internal modem, network card) and the RAM.

C) Random Access Memory or RAM

Stores information being used by the computer (temporary memory) Its quantity of memory in MB or GB Its speed in Mhz must be compatible with the motherboard RAM or random access memory is used to temporarily store information used by the computer when it is running. used. Thanks to RAM, the processor does its work much faster and more efficiently, because the cache improves data transmission between the processor and the RAM memory.

D) Hard disk (stores and reads information) ;

E) Peripherals Mouse (wired or infra-red)

F) Keyboard

G) Monitor (flat screen)

X.4.2. PROGRAMME TYPES

There are many programs and software that are important in computing. Some of the best known are operating systems such as **Windows** and **macOS,** office suites such as **Microsoft Office** and **LibreOffice**, web browsers such as **Google Chrome** and **Mozilla Firefox**, photo editing software such as Adobe **Photoshop,** video editing software such as **Adobe Première** and **Final Cut Pro,** and programming software such as **Java** and **Python.**

In conclusion, computing is a science that has radically changed our daily lives. It is based on discrete mathematics and can store and process vast quantities of information.

There are three types of software: system software, application software and development software.

Finally, the most important programmes and software in computing include operating systems, office suites, web browsers, photo editing software and programming software.

X.5. PREVENTIVE MAINTENANCE

X.5.1. COMPUTER HEALTH COMPROMISE FACTORS

a) Viruses and malware, the most common IT risks

Constantly evolving, viruses are software programmed to cause harm. They can physically attack workstations or act silently to retrieve sensitive information.

b) Fraudulent emails

More insidious than viruses, since they require human action on the part of the user, social engineering threats are attempts at piracy that are similar to fraud.

c) Piracy

Hackers gain access to an intermediate system through a security breach in the network or at one or more workstations. These IT risks are lower, but the consequences are much more serious. Best practice: deploy a complex password strategy and a new-generation firewall that is well configured and up to date. Call in an external service provider to carry out a Pentest audit (penetration test).

d) Industrial espionage

Industrial espionage carried out by a competitor or a hacker looking sell sensitive information can range from data corruption to patent theft, infringing the company's intellectual property. Best practice: remove access for former users (ex-employees) and create guest accounts with restricted rights for external parties (service providers).

e) Embezzlement

The majority of computer frauds take place in the workplace and can be perpetrated by your own employees. According to Ernst & Young, between 2009 and 2011, more than one in five companies worldwide was a victim. In this context, intrusion detection systems are not enough to protect you. Best practice: restrict access to confidential and sensitive files according to user profiles. Partition folders and resources by service, with authentication. Limit administrator rights to managers (IT Department).

f) Loss of confidential information

It can occur as a result of a hardware malfunction (server breakdown) or an error by your staff. Best practice: set up an effective backup system.

g) The handling error

Even if the error is human, poor handling can have serious consequences for your business. Best practice: train employees in the use of applications and software. Set up restore points so that an old version of files can be recovered.

X.5.2. PREVENTIVE MAINTENANCE PLAN

A **preventive maintenance** plan refers to all the actions planned to anticipate and reduce the probability of equipment failure: troubleshooting, replacement or overhaul. The aim of this proactive approach is to detect signs of a future breakdown at an early stage, so as to reduce the need for corrective maintenance.

Implementing a **preventive maintenance plan** has an impact on several aspects of your maintenance: productivity, profitability and safety.

Guaranteeing the reliability of the equipment for which you are responsible is part of assistance based on the prevention of technical incidents. Preventing or anticipating future equipment failures ensures stability for your organisation.

A maintenance strategy requires a certain amount of rigour if it is to be relevant. You need to understand what it is, why it's important and how to implement it.

X.5.3. TYPES OF PREVENTIVE MAINTENANCE

A. SYSTEMATIC PREVENTIVE MAINTENANCE

It consists staggering a maintenance cycle over a pre-established schedule, based on the estimated lifespan of the equipment, at a defined date and period.

B. CONDITION-BASED PREVENTIVE MAINTENANCE

Conditional maintenance is based on malfunction monitoring indicators: according to a precise parameter setting, reaching a certain level of failure triggers a maintenance intervention.

C. PREDICTIVE MAINTENANCE

It assesses the probabilities of future risks of deterioration of installations based on data transmitted by IoT sensors. This information determines monitoring parameters, alarm thresholds based on set reference values, the frequency of monitoring and replacement, etc.

CHAPTER XI

INTERNET[21]

XI.1. BACKGROUND

The first texts describing the social interactions that could be made possible by a computer network were a series of memos written by J.C.R. Licklider of MIT in August 1962 on his concept of a "galactic network". He imagined a set of globally interconnected computers through which anyone could quickly access data and programmes from any location. In theory, the concept was very similar to today' Internet. Licklider was the first head of DARPA[4] , 'scomputer research programmelaunched in October 1962. During his time at DARPA, he persuaded his successors, Ivan Sutherland, Bob Taylor and MIT researcher Lawrence G. Roberts, of the value of this computer network concept.

Leonard Kleinrock of MIT published the first paper on the use of packet switching in July 1961 and the first book on the subject in 1964. Kleinrock convinced Roberts of the theoretical realisation of communications using packet switching rather than dedicated circuits, which proved to be a major step towards computer networks. Another key step was to enable computers to communicate with each other. In 1965, explore this, with the help of Thomas Merrill, Roberts connected the TX-2 computer in Massachusetts with the Q-32 computer in California via a low-speed, switched telephone link, creating the first (albeit very small) network wide-area computer ever built. This experiment proved that time-sharing computers could work together very well, running programs and retrieving data as necessary from the remote machine, but that the dial-up telephone system was totally inadequate. Kleinrock's belief in the need for packet switching was confirmed.

At the end of 1966, Roberts was hired at DARPA to develop the computer network concept and quickly put in place his plan for the "ARPANET" network, which he published in 1967. At the conference where he presented the paper, a presentation on a packet-switched network concept was also given by Donald Davies and Roger Scantlebury of NPL in the UK. Scantlebury told Roberts about the work of NPL as well as that of Paul Baran and others at RAND. The RAND group had written a paper on the use of a packet-switched network for secure voice transmission in the military in

1964. As it happened, the work carried out at MIT (1961-1967), RAND (1962-1965) and NPL (1964-1967) all took place in parallel without any of the researchers being aware of the work of the others. The word "packet" was adopted from the work at NPL and the proposed transmission speed to be used in the design of ARPANET was improved from 2.4 kbps to 50 kbps.

In August 1968, having refined the general structure and specifications of the ARPANET network, Roberts and DARPA launched a call for tenders for the production of a key component of the network: packet switches called Interface Message Processors (IMPs). Bolt Beranek and Newman (BBN), headed by Frank Heart, won the tender in December 1968. While the BBN team worked on the IMPs with Bob Kahn, playing a key role in the architectural design of the ARPANET network, the network topology and economics were designed and optimised by Roberts, who worked with Howard Frank and his team at Network Analysis Corporation, and the network measurement system was prepared by Professor Kleinrock's team at UCLA.

Thanks to Kleinrock's early development of packet switching theory and his focus on analysis, design and measurement, his Network Measurement Center at UCLA was chosen to be the first node on the ARPANET. In September 1969, BBN installed the first IMP network equipment at UCLA and the first host computer was connected to it. Doug Engelbart's Augmenting Human Intelligence project (which included the first hypertext system, NLS) at the Stanford Research Institute (SRI) provided a second nreud. The SRI supported the Network Information Center, headed by Elizabeth (Jake) Feinler and including functions such as maintaining tables of hostnames and addresses and a directory of RFCs.

A month later, when SRI was connected to the ARPANET network, the first host-to-host message was sent from Kleinrock's laboratory to SRI. Two more nodes were added at UC Santa Barbara (UCSB) and the University of Utah. These latter two nodes incorporated application visualisation projects, with Glen Culler and Burton Fried at UCSB investigating methods for displaying mathematical functions using memory screens to cope with the refresh problem on the network, and Robert Taylor and Ivan Sutherland the University of Utah investigating methods for 3D representations on the network. By the end of 1969, the initial ARPANET network consisted of four host computers and the Internet was born. Even at this early stage, it's worth noting that network research integrated both work on the underlying network and work on how to use the network. This tradition continues to this day.

Computers were quickly added to the ARPANET network over the next few years, and work continued on completing a functionally complete host-to-host communications protocol and other network software. In December 1970, the Network Working Group (NWG), led by S. Crocker, completed the host-to-host communications protocol for the ARPANET, called the Network Control Protocol or NCP. As ARPANET sites finished implementing NCP between 1971 and 1972, network users were finally able to develop the first applications.

In October 1972, Kahn organised a major and very successful demonstration of the ARPANET network at the International Conference on Computer Communications (ICCC). It was the first public demonstration of this new technology. It was also in 1972 that the first major application was developed: electronic mail. In March, Ray Tomlinson at BBN wrote the first basic software for sending and receiving electronic mailmeeting the communication needs of ARPANET developers. In July, Roberts extended his application by writing the first e-mail program to list, selectively read, classify, route and reply messages. From there, e-mail took off as most pervasive network application for over a decade. It was a harbinger of the kind of activity we see on the World Wide Web today - the huge growth in traffic of all kinds linking people together.

XI.2. DEFINITION

This is a set of interconnected global networks that enable computers and servers to communicate efficiently using a common communications protocol (IP). [21]

XI.3 ACCESS TO THE INTERNET (Word Wide Web)

There are two ways of connecting to the Internet: wired and wireless. Wired connections use physical cables to connect to the internet, while wireless connections use radio waves. Wired connections are generally faster and more reliable than wireless connections, but they also require cables and can be difficult to install. Wireless connections, on the other hand, are more practical and easier to install, but can be slower and less reliable.

XI.4. BROWSER (INTERNET EXPLORER, MOZILLA, OPERA, ETC.)

A browser is used to **view Internet pages,** which contain text, images, videos, links and other functions. A browser connects to serversweb , which send it the code from websites and transform it into a graphical web page.

---

[21] https://www.insee.fr/, consulted on 27/09/2023 at 15:49'.

There are several different browsers, including Internet Explorer, Firefox, Safari and Chrome. A browser is a window onto all human knowledge, allowing to yousearch for the answer to any question.

XI.5. SEARCH ENGINES (GOOGLE,...)

A **search engine** is, as its name suggests, a tool that allows you to search the Web (or a personal computer) for resources, content, documents, etc., using keywords.

All you have to do is enter the expressions that make up your query, and the **search engine** will automatically find the resources that match your search. The results are organised according to the logic of each search engine.

BIBLIOGRAPHY

- **The works**

1. Curriculum national des Humanités Techniques Commerciales, Option: Secrétariat-administration ;
2. CAZES and J. DELACROIX, *Architecture des machines et des systèmes informatiques*, 3e edition, Paris, Dunod, 2008;
3. CHANTAL MORLY, *Management d'un projet système d'information. Principles*, techniques,
4. ORACLE and TECH TARGET, *Le rôle de l'informatique dans l'entreprise*, s. l, Ed. TechTargetcustomer Media ;
5. TANENBAUM, *Systèmes d'exploitation, 3ème édition*, Paris, Pearson ;

- **The websites**

1. www.insee.fr/
2. www.internetsociety.org
3. www.futura-sciences.com
4. www.larousse.fr
5. www.blog-du-net.net
6. www.google.com
7. www.toupie.org/Dictionnaire/Information.htm
8. http://web.undp.org
9. www.lemagit.fr
10. www.labri.fr
11. www.yourtopia.fr
12. https://konfuzio.com

MIX
Papier aus verantwortungsvollen Quellen
Paper from responsible sources
FSC® C105338

Printed by Books on Demand GmbH, Norderstedt / Germany